Domestic Violence Perpetrators

52 Week

Intervention Program

Compiled by: Sharie Stines, PsyD,

August 2017

Domestic Violence Intervention Program: Outline Of General Group Topics And Activities

Introduction

This book contains a curriculum for leading 52 weeks of domestic violence perpetrator's groups for men. Each lesson is designed to provide content for a two-hour group and includes group discussion and applicable homework.

Studies have shown that group Batterer's Intervention Programs (BIPs) do have a positive impact on the recidivism rate of violence. Further analysis has also indicated that the types of approaches that are most effective utilize Cognitive Behavior Therapy (CBT) and Motivational Interviewing (MI) (Edleson, 2012).

Cognitive Behavior Therapy is time-sensitive, structured, present-oriented psychotherapy directed toward solving current problems and teaching clients skills to modify dysfunctional thinking and behavior (Beck Institute, n.d.).Motivational Interviewing seeks to elicit the client's concerns and thoughts while providing non-judgmental feedback on discrepant behaviors. This book attempts to provide both CBT and MI type interventions.

The following is a list of content within the lessons provided in this manual:

- Definitions Of Violence
- Cycle Of Violence
- Managing Anger
- Effects On Children And Family
- Emotional Intelligence
- Substance Abuse
- Cultural Issues
- Defensive Mechanisms
- Treatment Options
- Cognitive Distortions
- Grief Recovery
- Boundaries
- Empathy
- Much more!

Each lesson contains thoughtful group discussion material and self-application homework. Everything you need to run groups for a 52 week batterer's intervention program for men can be found in this volume. We have also included sample group rules and progress notes for your use.

For suggestions and ideas for improvement, please email the editor at: therecoveryexpert@gmail.com

Tips For Running An Effective Group

- **Develop A Check-In Process During Each Group:** Ask all group members to briefly state how they are feeling and what they want from the particular session. Listen to what group members have to say during the check-in time. This should be quick. You could ask a couple of questions, such as, "How do you feel about being here today?" or, "Do you have any thoughts or feelings about our last group session?"

- **Define Group Goals:** As the leader of the group, determine what your goals for the group are, and ask each individual group member what his or her goals are for participating in the group.

- **Help Group Members Define Personal Goals:** Many times group members have very vague goals for themselves. Your job as the leader is to help members translate these vague ideas into clear and workable goals. This is to be done collaboratively, between you and the group members.

- **Be A Good Role Model:** One important thing to keep in mind as a group leader is that your job is to be a healthy role model to group members. Help create a climate of trust within the group and between group members. Also, be psychologically present during group session.

- **Listen And Attend To Group Members:** Make sure you listen as each group member speaks. Do not interrupt or give advice. Wait until group member has finished speaking before you give feedback and try to encourage rather than lecture.

- **Be Respectful:** Avoid critical judgments and labels. Express warmth and support rather than indifference to group members and co-leaders.

- **Maintain Trust:** Ensure that the group maintains a sense of safety. Develop a healthy atmosphere so that each member feels safe and make sure you have a plan for any behaviors that hurt group members. Continue to establish trust in the group by setting appropriate boundaries for group members.

- **Encourage All Group Members To Be Active Participants In Group:** Some participants in your group may resist speaking, and while it is true that something can be gained by observation, remind silent group members that their growth will be limited, and that others will never get to know them if they do not make an effort to actively participate in group process.

- **Avoid Too Much Teaching:** Too much emphasis on teaching in the group can have a negative influence on the group process. Encourage group participation and discussion. This helps build group cohesion and discourages dependence on the leader for personal growth.

- **Assign Homework:** Even if your homework involves the simple statement, "apply what you learned this week," and "discuss how you did with your homework over the past week." Require your clients to think about the concepts and use the concepts taught in their daily lives. Having clients practice new behaviors is the most effective way to teach.

Goals For Batterer's Intervention Program

(Excerpted from: Emerge Abuser Education Program Group Goals)

- Immediately stop physical abuse, bullying behaviors, covert abuse, intimidation, or any other types of abusive attitudes and behaviors.

- Recognize and describe how you have been harmful towards your partner and family.

- Understand the harm this behavior has caused.

- Develop an understanding of how you have benefited from your behavior in the past and how you can benefit from changing your behavior now.

- Work to be open and honest with group leaders and fellow group members.

- Be able to identify ongoing harmful behavior.

- Be able to stop comparing your current behavior to past behavior that was more harmful.

- Examine what you need to do to become respectful and non-abusive.

- Participate during group discussions.

- Give feedback to fellow group members.

- Demonstrate respect to fellow group members and group leaders.

- Identify what is the most helpful feedback for you to hear from others.

- Work to develop empathy for your partner and make amends for harm you've caused.

- Develop a personal recovery plan for changing your damaging beliefs, attitudes, and behaviors.

- Be willing to be held accountable by other group members and group leaders.

Group Rules

1. We will begin and end each meeting on time. Please try to be on time to the group.

2. Keep everything heard in this group meeting confidential. What is shared in the group stays in the group.

3. Practice good listening skills. Listen to each other and give each person time to share without interruption.

4. Share your experiences and feelings, but not your advice.

5. Be respectful and sensitive to each other.

6. Stay off your phone during group sessions.

7. Be supportive and encouraging to each other.

8. Do not monopolize the discussion. Share your thoughts in three minutes or less and be mindful of others.

9. Avoid criticism. Do not put down other people in the group.

10. Take responsibility for yourself. Take the focus off of others' problems, and use group topic for your own personal growth.

11. Do not interrupt while others are speaking. Please wait for your turn.

12. Each person is responsible for making this group work.

WEEKLY BIP PROGRESS NOTES

GROUP DAY: MON TUE WED THUR FRI SAT   **GROUP TIME:** _____

Client Name: _____   **Facilitator:** _____

Group Topic: _____ **Group #:** _____ **Date:** _____

PARTICIPATION: □ ACTIVE □ QUIET □ NEEDS PROMPTING □ DEFENSIVE □ CLOSED □ SUPERFICIAL

BEHAVIOR:
□ COOPERATIVE □ ENTHUSIASTIC □ OPEN TO LEARNING
□ RESISTANT □ HOSTILE □ DENYING
□ BLAMING □ MINIMIZING

PROGRESS: □ EXCELLENT □ POSITIVE □ FAIR □ NEGATIVE □ UNACCEPTABLE □ UNCERTAIN

ADDITIONAL INFORMATION: Verbalizes responsibility for abuse? □ YES □ NO
Avoids derogatory/abusive language in group? □ YES □ NO
Made payment for session? □ YES □ NO
Reports using skills learned (i.e., time outs)? □ YES □ NO

COMMENTS (if necessary): _____Missed # _____ □ N/A

FACILITATOR'S SIGNATURE: _____

Group Topic: _____ **Group #:** _____ **Date:** _____

PARTICIPATION: □ ACTIVE □ QUIET □ NEEDS PROMPTING □ DEFENSIVE □ CLOSED □ SUPERFICIAL

BEHAVIOR:
□ COOPERATIVE □ ENTHUSIASTIC □ OPEN TO LEARNING
□ RESISTANT
□ HOSTILE □ DENYING □ BLAMING □ MINIMIZING

PROGRESS: □ EXCELLENT □ POSITIVE □ FAIR □ NEGATIVE □ UNACCEPTABLE □ UNCERTAIN

ADDITIONAL INFORMATION: Verbalizes responsibility for abuse? □ YES □ NO
Avoids derogatory/abusive language in group? □ YES □ NO
Made payment for session? □ YES □ NO
Reports using skills learned (i.e., time outs)? □ YES □ NO

COMMENTS (if necessary): _____Missed # _____ □ N/A

FACILITATOR'S SIGNATURE: _____

Group Topic: _____ **Group #:** _____ **Date:** _____

PARTICIPATION: □ ACTIVE □ QUIET □ NEEDS PROMPTING □ DEFENSIVE □ CLOSED □ SUPERFICIAL

BEHAVIOR:
□ COOPERATIVE □ ENTHUSIASTIC □ OPEN TO LEARNING
□ RESISTANT
□ HOSTILE □ DENYING □ BLAMING □ MINIMIZING

PROGRESS: □ EXCELLENT □ POSITIVE □ FAIR □ NEGATIVE □ UNACCEPTABLE □ UNCERTAIN

ADDITIONAL INFORMATION: Verbalizes responsibility for abuse? □ YES □ NO
Avoids derogatory/abusive language in group? □ YES □ NO
Made payment for session? □ YES □ NO
Reports using skills learned (i.e., time outs)? □ YES □ NO

COMMENTS (if necessary): _____Missed # _____ □ N/A

FACILITATOR'S SIGNATURE: _____

Lesson 1: Identifying Warning Signs

Common Warning Signs Of Domestic Violence

The following list can help you determine whether you or someone you care about is involved in an abusive relationship. Not all of these characteristics need to be present for a relationship to be abusive, and characteristics by themselves do not necessarily indicate abuse.

Think about your own beliefs, attitudes and behaviors. Can you see yourself demonstrating any of the following?

- Believe you have the right to dictate your partner's behavior, privileges, responses and opinions.

- Demonstrate ownership of your partner or extreme possessiveness. Do you say things like, "I can't live without you," or "You are my whole world."

- You blame your partner for your problems or behavior.

- Isolate your partner – don't allow your partner to see family or friends.

- Constantly need to know your partner's whereabouts and expect him/her to spend all of his/her free time with you.

- Humiliate your partner in public.

- Force your partner to have sex or perform sexual acts.

- Insist on controlling the money – both yours and his/hers.

- Refuse to let your partner go to work or force him/her to work.

- Have no regard for your partner's physical or mental health.

- Criticize your partner's appearance, weight, clothes, etc.

- Pressure your partner to live together or get married before he/she is ready to do so.

- Is easily angered.

- Become angry when your partner has a different opinion than you.

- You do not take your partner's advice, rarely if ever.

- Do you show jealousy toward your partner's children, family, friends, or job?

- Do you tell your partner things that cause him/her to fear the ending of the relationship?

- You demonstrate Dr. Jekyll/Mr. Hyde behaviors, such as being charming in public and aggressive in private.

- Display violent behavior toward other people.

- Disregard the law; feel that you are above the law and rules don't apply to you.

- Do not want your partner to know about your past.

- Blame your past relationship problems on your ex-partner.

- Have a history of domestic violence

Writing Assignment:

Go through each point above and write a personal example of how you have used each in your relationship(s), both in the past and in the present. Write about your actions, beliefs, and emotions.

Next, if you notice a pattern or see an area that needs to change, develop a recovery plan for yourself regarding what you need to change.

Lesson 2: Cycle Of Abuse

(Excerpted from: CCWRC Women's Resource Center

What is Domestic Violence?

The term **"domestic violence"** refers to a range of abusive behaviors ranging from degrading remarks and cruel jokes, threatening looks, constant monitoring, economic exploitation, punches and kicks, sexual abuse, and homicide. All of these tactics are used by abusers to gain power and control over their victims. Unchecked, domestic violence almost always increases in frequency and severity.

Domestic Violence Comes In Many Forms, Including:

- Physical Abuse

- Verbal Abuse

- Emotional Abuse

- Sexual Abuse

- Financial Abuse

- Stalking

Many victims suffer all forms of abuse. Verbal and emotional abuse may be more subtle than physical harm, but this doesn't mean it is less destructive to victims. Many have said that the emotional scars take much longer to heal than broken bones.

Who are the victims and who are the perpetrators?

Research shows that the overwhelming majority (about 95%) of adult victims of domestic violence are women. Although the "norm" of domestic violence in relationships is "male perpetrator and female victim", anyone can be a victim of abuse.

Domestic violence occurs regardless of race, age, socioeconomic status, sexual orientation, mental or physical ability or religious background.

Abusers are not easily identifiable. While their behaviors may seem pathological, they are not likely to suffer from severe mental disorders. Domestic violence is **NOT** caused by mental illness, alcohol abuse, or stress. It is caused by one person's desire to have power and control over a partner and it is a choice to behave in this way. Batterers frequently make excuses for their violence, claiming loss of control due to alcohol or drug use, or extreme stress. **Although drug and alcohol abuse may intensify existing violent behavior, it does not cause domestic violence.**

Abusers typically follow a pattern called the Cycle of Abuse. The cycle can occur hundreds of times in an abusive relationship, the total cycle taking anywhere from a few hours, to a year or more to complete. However, the length of the cycle usually diminishes over time so that the "reconciliation" and "calm" stages may disappear.

Why do victims of abuse stay?

Many people struggle with the fact that a victim may not leave their abuser. While it may seem like a simple decision to those outside the relationship, victims of abuse often face multiple barriers to leaving, including:

- Financial dependence

- Desire to keep family together

- Hope that the abuse will stop

- Pressure from family

- Denial

- Shame

- Lack of resources

- FEAR

Many people believe that victims of domestic violence will be safe once they separate from their abusers. They also believe that victims are free to leave abusers at any time. However, leaving does not usually put an end to the violence. Abusers often escalate their violence to coerce a victim into reconciliation or to retaliate for the victim's rejection or abandonment of the abuser.

Abusers who believe they are entitled to a relationship with thevictims or that they "own" their partners view a victim's leaving as the ultimate betrayal and will likely retaliate. Because of this, leaving an abusive relationship can be very dangerous. Individuals are most likely to be murdered when attempting to report abuse or leave an abusive relationship.

This does not mean the victims should stay. Living with an abuser is highly dangerous because the violence usually escalates and becomes more frequent over time.

Statistics

- On average, nearly 20 people per minute are physically abused by an intimate partner in the United States. During one year, this equates to more than 10 million women and men.

- 1 in 3 women and 1 in 4 men have been victims of [some form of] physical violence by an intimate partner within their lifetime.

- 1 in 5 women and 1 in 7 men have been victims of severe physical violence by an intimate partner in their lifetime.

- 1 in 7 women and 1 in 18 men have been stalked by an intimate partner during their lifetime to the point to which they felt very fearful, or believed that they or someone close to them would be harmed or killed.

- On a typical day, there are more than 20,000 phone calls placed to domestic violence hotlines nationwide.

- The presence of a gun in a domestic violence situation increases the risk of homicide by 500%.

- Intimate partner violence accounts for 15% of all violent crimes.

- Women between the ages of 18-24 are most commonly abused by an intimate partner.

- 19% of domestic violence involves a weapon.

- Domestic victimization is correlated with a higher rate of depression and suicidal behavior.

- Only 34% of people who are injured by intimate partners receive medical care for their injuries.

Understanding the Cycle of Violence – Information for Law Enforcement

Source: Los Angeles Police Department (lapdonline.org)

Domestic violence relationships exhibit certain characteristics that differ from healthy, intimate relationships. Understanding the difference may be the key to recognizing the need to seek assistance.

Violent relationships usually do not begin with violence. Like normal, healthy couples, they begin with romance.

1.   Romance

During this time, the batterer attempts to bond or connect with their partner. Domestic violence relationships never return to romance once the cycle begins. Domestic violence partners then proceed into the next phase of the Cycle of Violence, called the Tension Building Phase, which is marked by Power and Control.

2.   Tension Building Phase

The batterer begins to assert his or her power over the victim in an attempt to control the victim's actions. Batterers will set rules for the victim; that are impossible to follow. They will tell the victim that there will be consequences if they break the rules. Sadly, the consequences usually result in violence against the victim. Rules often may include; no contact with family members, money spending rules and/or needing to obtain permission for everything the victim does. Batterers use demeaning, degrading and derogatory phrases toward the victim in an attempt to "objectify" the victim. This is done because it is easier to commit violence against an "object" rather than someone you are supposed to love.

The victim may internalize the appropriate anger at the abuser's unfairness and experience physical effects such as depression, tension, anxiety and headaches. As the tension in the relationship increases, minor episodes of violence increase, such as pinching, slapping or shoving.

The rules are nearly impossible to follow, but victims try to follow them in an attempt to forestall the inevitable assaults. The violation of the rules leads the couple into the next phase, Acute Battering Phase.

3.   Acute Battering Incident

During this phase, the batterer exhibits uncontrolled violent outbursts. This is the shortest of the three, but the most dangerous. Batterers decide to teach the victim a lesson and will usually injure the victim. The injuries may start out as minor such as a slap, a pinch, or hair pulling. As the cycle continues the violence becomes increasingly brutal and escalates into a great bodily injury or death.

If death does not occur, the victims usually react with shock, denial or disbelief and the cycle continues into the third phase The Acute Battering Phase ends in an explosion of violence. The victim may or may not fight back. Following the battering, the victim is in a state of physical and psychological shock. The batterer may discount the episode and underestimate the victim's injuries.

4.   Remorseful Phase

During this last phase of the cycle of violence, the batterer usually begins an intense effort to win forgiveness and ensure that the relationship will not break up. Batterers ask for forgiveness, say it will not happen again, and behave in a very loving and kind manner. While batterers apologize, they still blame the victim for the violence stating, "If you had only stayed home like I asked you, I wouldn't have had to hit you..." or "I'll never do it again..." Often batterers use gifts to convince the victim to forgive. The victim wants to believe that the abuse will end.

The victims' feelings that the abuse will now stop is supported by the batterer's loving behavior.

Once violence has begun, it continues to increase in both frequency and severity. When you identify the cycle of violence in your relationship or that of a loved one, you can start to see how you or your friend have been victimized. Change cannot occur unless you seek assistance from a trained professional. Remember life is not so lacking in value that it should be risked in order to "help" someone who is brutally being battered.

One who has never experienced repeated abuse over a long period of time will find it difficult to understand why a victim of abuse remains in the abusive relationship. These are common reactions from those untrained in abuse: "Why doesn't she just leave? No one is stopping her. She must be a very weak person or she would."

To maintain power and control, an abuser will wear down the self-esteem and self-reliance of his victim. Over time the victim actually believes she is worthless and incapable of doing anything on her own. Therefore, it is very significant when a woman does try to leave an abusive environment. On average, a victim of abuse will leave and return seven times before permanently leaving.

Lesson 3: The Drama Triangle

Using the Karpman Triangle (or Drama Triangle) as a guide, here is a summary of the process of "recovery" from manipulative relationship dynamics. In case you aren't familiar with the Karpman Triangle, it represents the dynamics of unhealthy and manipulative relationships. Each corner of the triangle depicts a role we play in the game of a dysfunctional relationship.

One corner is the victim (please help me); one corner is the rescuer (the over-responsible, controller); and the other corner is the persecutor (the villain, the bully, the superior one). The victim usually "hooks" the other person into becoming a rescuer and if the victim role fails, he may switch roles into becoming the persecutor as a more overt means of accomplishing the goal. People can often switch roles, playing the part of each one, all in one dramatic interaction. You will often find these relationship dynamics at play in families with addictions and abuse.

(Karpman Drama Triangle; Source: www.choiceconflictresolution.com)

Here are some steps to take to overcome participating in unhealthy interactions with others:

1. Realize that you are repeating a pattern. Stand back and observe your pattern. Most likely you are being triggered in some way, or manipulated by someone close to you. In order to change the pattern, you need to see what it is first. Once you are aware of your part, play a different tune. Sing a new song. Don't do the same thing you have always done. Take a contrary action.

2. Under any circumstance, do not become defensive. Keep a neutral attitude. Even if you feel defensive (especially if you feel defensive) do not act from that vantage point. Use a non-reactive, non-emotional, easy going tone. Make statements that stop the conflict, for instance, use terms like, "Perhaps you're right." "That could be." "Interesting point." "Nevertheless…" Remind yourself to not get "hooked" into the drama.

3. If you find yourself feeling like a victim, learn to take responsibility for yourself, not blaming others for how your life is turning out. Even if you truly are the victim, do not conclude that you are powerless to take care of yourself in the situation. Take the energy you feel about being victimized and turn it in to **determination**. Resolve to yourself that you will figure out how to solve your problem without the other person's help. This will help you develop your own personal power.

4. If you find yourself feeling like you're taking on too much responsibility, back off, allowing others to take on their own responsibilities, even allowing others to fail if that is what happens. Sometimes others need to face consequences for their own choices. Remind yourself that you are not responsible for other people's choices – even if that person is your child. Also, realize that everyone has a right to **personal agency** – that is the right to determine their own destiny (God willing). It is more healthy for a parent to let a child learn the hard way than to jump in and fix everything for him. This goes for other types of relationships as well. Allow the other person the dignity to figure out their own life. Remember this, when you rescue another person: you are sending them the implied message that they are too incompetent to do it themselves.

5. Refrain from the following: blaming, criticizing, accusing, lecturing, scolding, monitoring, threatening, preaching, obsessing, over-reacting, or under-reacting. Instead, focus on being neutral. Ask yourself, "How can I bring a blessing to this situation? Or, how can I be a soothing presence right now?" If the other person is unwilling or unable to participate in a healthy interaction, figure out a way to remove yourself physically from the encounter until a safer time.

6. Remember the term **FOG**. **FOG** stands for *Fear, Obligation, Guilt*. If you feel any of those feelings, consistently, in a significant relationship, you are most likely dealing with a manipulator. You need to remember to **get out of the FOG**. Do not allow yourself to be manipulated. On the other hand, if you are trying to make another person feel consistently Fearful, Obligated, or Guilty, you are the manipulator and are not operating with emotional health. Change. Be direct, honest, and live with integrity.

7. Realize that when a person is living in active addiction and abuse, you will not be able to have a healthy relationship with the person until he or she, too, is in a real process of recovery. If the person is a recovering alcoholic, he will be sober and working an actual program. If the person is a recovering abuser, he will be seeking help from accountability partners and will actually be introspective and thoughtful. If your loved one is not healthy, don't think you can have a healthy relationship with that person. The best thing you can do is just focus on your own emotional growth. Remember, recovery is for those who want it, not for those who need it.

Lesson 4: Your First Steps Toward Change (Part 1)

(Excerpted from L. Bancroft's Guide for Change (Part 1) (n.d.)

Becoming a responsible, kind relationship partner has some similarities to learning to play a musical instrument, or learning to speak a new language. You think at first, "I couldn't possibly do that—you're expecting way too much from me." The person who has been abusing substances, or chronically mistreating his partner, or running away from his mental health problems, says, "You can't expect me to change that much — you're asking me to be a completely different person! I am who I am!"

So if your partner is demanding that you change the way you treat her, you may feel that she is making unfair demands on you, and that you're being assigned a task that you shouldn't be stuck with. **These are the voices in your head that don't want you to grow**; they'd rather keep making excuses and blaming the other person, which seems so much easier.

But on your better days, when you are being honest with yourself, you know that your partner is right; you can't blame your behavior or your other problems on her, and it's time to get on with making changes. And learning to behave responsibly, maturely, and non-abusively doesn't involve giving up who you "really" are — unless you're trying to argue that you are "really" a selfish, demeaning, intimidating person! I'm confident you don't want to make that argument. When you view the situation with clarity, there's no excuse not to get down to the business of working on yourself. So do it.

The process of change is difficult but it's not mysterious. You begin at the beginning and learn what you need to learn, one piece at a time, just as the aspiring musician has to.

Your first task is to examine the attitudes that you take toward your partner's grievances. From there we will move on to **overcoming denial**, **stopping your retaliatory behaviors**, **making a plan**, and **connecting yourself to positive influences**. These steps are the beginnings of the change process.

THE FIRST STEPS TOWARD CHANGE

1. Changing your attitude toward your partner's complaints.

2. Understanding your denial, and coming out of it.

3. Stopping your retaliations against your partner for raising grievances.

4. Making a plan.

5. Connecting to positive influences for growth and change. I will take you through each step in detail, describing the work you need to do on each one.

STEP ONE: Changing what you tell yourself about the issues the other person raises

I am going to assume that the fact that you are reading this guide to change means that your partner has been complaining about certain aspects of your behavior for a long time (whether you have been hearing it or not). Her grievances may include that you spend more time with your drinking buddies than you do with her, or that you're too rough during sex, or you pressure her to do things sexually that she doesn't find appealing, or that you stick her with all the housework and child care, or that you insult her and act like you think you're better than she is.

So far, your internal messages about her complaints — we might call it your "self- talk" — have largely been that she doesn't know what she's talking about, or that she's making something out of nothing, or that there's something wrong with her. If these weren't your internal messages, you would have improved your behavior long ago. You have developed an elaborate set of internal messages that discredit your partner's perspective, to convince yourself that you don't need to take her complaints seriously.

Observe your own thinking over the next couple of weeks; you'll notice that you repeat these negative beliefs about her to yourself over and over, almost like a chant, as if you were trying to keep yourself convinced. So here's the first point to focus on: whatever she has been raising with you; you haven't been hearing it, and as a result, you haven't done anything meaningful to take care of the problems your behavior has created. Fortunately, it isn't too late.

Here are examples of the kinds of situations that may occur in your "self-talk," your inner world of recurring *unhealthy* messages:

"She's just trying to control me like a mother, that's why she won't stop bugging me."

"She doesn't know how to have a good time, so she doesn't want me to have a good time."

"She's just determined to find something wrong with every little thing I do."

"She just doesn't understand men. She wants me to be like a woman."

"She ignores all the good things I do, and just notices the bad things."

"She's stupid, she doesn't know anything."

"She's fucking crazy, there's no reason to listen to her."

"She just likes to get on my case because she's a bitch."

"I've worked so hard on changing, and she just doesn't appreciate it."

And the list could go on with similar attitudes. Discrediting her is your ticket to running away from yourself. As you read the list above, you may find yourself in an internal argument. On one hand you may tell yourself, "I don't have any of those attitudes," and on the other you may think, "Of course I think that about her, because it's true." Both reactions will keep you from really looking. So work to drop defensive habits and look honestly at what's been going on.

Homework:

For the next few weeks, pay close attention to the negative messages you collect about your partner. When she brings up a complaint, a criticism, or a step that she is asking you to take, listen carefully to the grievance or request and do not discredit it. When you are alone, write down the points she was making, and spend some time trying to take them in.

Notice the messages that go through your head about why her issue does not have to be taken seriously. In order to break your habit of self-talk that discredits your partner, start replacing the negative messages with appropriate ones, chanting (internally) the good ones rather than the bad ones as you try to reexamine your perspective. Examples of appropriate *healthy* self-talk include:

"She has the right to bring grievances."

"She has the right to be angry with me."

"She has built up a lot of bad feeling because of things I've done in the past, and I need to accept that and give her room for those feelings."

"She is trying to make our relationship work better."

"She needs me to make changes so that I stop hurting her (and the kids)."

"Her complaints are (at least) as valid as mine are."

"I can deal with this issue, instead of shooting her down."

"She's a good person, and she knows what she's talking about."

"How do I want her to feel about me twenty minutes from now? What do I need to do differently to bring that about?"

Work daily on changing your self-talk habits, replacing your destructive attitudes with constructive, respectful ones.

Lesson 5: Your First Steps Toward Change (Part 2): Learning To Really Hear The Other Person

(Excerpted from L. Bancroft's Guide For Change (Part 1) (n.d.)

Really listen to what your partner is saying

Deciding to take in the other person's side of arguments, and deciding to actually digest what her complaints have been requires that you not only listen well but that you **stop making yourself into the victim**.

For example, you have to stop acting like it's such a burden to take her opinion seriously; after all, you certainly expect her to take your opinions seriously, including your complaints. So why do you start to act so victimized when she has a grievance? Because playing "poor me" is a lot easier than looking at how bad your partner feels and what you need to do differently.

So when she is expressing her feelings, including her hurt or outrage, here's what to do:

- **Make a serious, careful effort to understand what she is saying, even if you think you already know**. You have a history in this relationship of listening poorly and assuming the worst, which **you can only correct by shutting your mouth and opening your mind**.

- **Respond in a thoughtful, fair way that does not include any insults or put-downs, do not accuse her of bad motives, and do not exaggerate or twist what she has just said.** Your response, even if you disagree with her, has to demonstrate that you are actually engaging seriously with the points she is making.

Sentences that begin with "oh, so what you're really saying is . . ." are off-limits. So are:

"you're just bringing this up because . . ."

"you're just mad because . . ."

"what this is really about is . . ."

** Do more good thinking on your own about what she has said, after the argument or discussion is over. The digestion process should continue for hours or even days.

You should be coming back to her later saying things like:

"I've been thinking over what you were saying and I realize you were really making sense."

"I'm sorry I was so defensive, and I'm ready now to take in what you were trying to tell me."

"I've thought about it and I can see why my actions weren't fair, and I'm sorry. I'll make a concerted effort not to do that again" (in reference to whatever her grievance was).

- **Don't bring up *your* complaints about her when she is in the midst of trying to raise *her* issues about you.** If you want to talk about your grievances, you need to bring them up another time. Another way of stating this point is that you need to stop deflecting the discussion from her concerns onto yours, which is an evasive tactic and often becomes an excuse to be nasty.

- **Don't require her to bring up her grievances in a perfect way.** If you don't like the way she is talking to you, you can bring that up with her later, but don't use it in the middle of an argument as an excuse to shut her off and not deal with what she is raising.

This last point leads to another important understanding for your work, one that you will have to focus on for at least 2-3 years and probably longer:

You have had habits of focusing on *your* feelings and *her* behavior. You have to completely shift the focus onto *her* feelings and *your* behavior.

And this means, for example, that you have to stop jumping on her about the tone she speaks to you in, but you're going to have to take it seriously when it's the other way around and she's complaining about *your* tone. And this is going to feel unfair to you, but actually it isn't unfair at all; it's an inevitable part of the process of overcoming your abusiveness.

Now, look back at the starred list above and ask yourself, "is this really such an unreasonable set of demands? Is this really a huge, unfair burden to put on a person? Do these requirements tie my hands so that I can't stand up for myself?" The answer is clearly no; attachment to the above behaviors is about being attached to *silencing her*. And your most urgent task is to stop silencing her.

Homework

Write down a few examples of ways in which you have retaliated against your partner or put up roadblocks when she was trying to raise concerns or express her anger to you. Then write down alternate ways you could have responded, drawing from the list above. Next, write some examples of disrespectful messages that you have been running inside your head as an excuse to blow her off when she's mad at you. Then write down a couple of positive attitudes toward her, and toward conflict that you will work to keep in mind instead, drawing from the list of positive messages above.

Lesson 6: Your First Steps Toward Change (Part 3): No More Going Ballistic

(Excerpted from L. Bancroft's Guide For Change (Part 1) (n.d.)

If there are certain subjects that you are extremely "touchy" about, so that you explode angrily or storm out of the room if she attempts to bring them up, that behavior has to stop. (**And yes, going ballistic is a choice; you are not forced to "lose it"** because she brings up a difficult topic, you are choosing to do so.)

Your partner gets to raise whatever issues she believes need to be addressed, and you are perfectly capable of dealing with it even if the subject is an upsetting one for you.

So these are the new rules if you are serious about changing your behavior:

- **You can't make any subjects out-of-bounds anymore**. She is permitted to raise any subject she wants to, and you can't scream, tell her to shut up, or get her back for it later. You don't get to tell her that she can't talk about issues that may have a big impact on her life- that is a denial of her basic rights. So it's time to deal.

- **The very fact that certain subjects are that volatile for you is a warning sign that you are running away from yourself,** whether it's an addiction, a mental health problem, or some other issue you are avoiding confronting.

I'm going to talk for a moment about a hypothetical controlling man. We'll call him Justin. Let's say that Justin's mother was an alcoholic, the kind that drank until she passed out on the floor of the hallway. Justin's partner is now finding that Justin has become quite a drinker himself, and it's causing problems for her. But when she tries to bring up how upset she is by how much he drinks, Justin comes unglued and starts to yell things like, "you don't know anything about alcohol abuse! I handle my alcohol just fine! I'm not passing out, I'm not driving drunk, I'm holding down a job! You should have been there when my mom was throwing up drunk and calling me a stinking little shit! I can't believe you are telling me I drink too much; you know how that makes me feel! Leave me the hell alone!!"

What Justin is refusing to look at (among other things) is that his drinking is having a bad impact on his partner and on his children; **he is acting as though this issue is just about him, but it isn't**. (He's also ignoring the reality that drinking problems take different forms, and that the fact that he doesn't drink the way his mother did proves nothing.) It is undoubtedly true that his memories of his mother's alcoholism are a great source of pain for him. It is also obvious, though, that another part of why the subject sets him off so much is that he realizes on some level that he is getting sucked down the same awful road that his mother went down, but he wants to pretend it isn't happening.

The overarching point is that Justin has to come out of the self-centered place that he has locked himself into and start considering his partner's feelings. And you need to do the same.

STEP TWO: owning up that you have a problem

It's been said a million times but I'm going to say it again: **people can't solve problems that they don't believe they have**. As long as you keeps insisting that your partner is exaggerating the problem, or she's too sensitive, or she just likes to get on your case, or she's actually the one "who is messed up," you can't progress.

What comes up for you when you try to make room for the possibility that you really do need to get help, and do need to change? Perhaps first you feel ashamed to admit that she has been right all along, given that you have been so hotly and disparagingly telling her how wrong she is. You may feel that you're a bad person for having this problem.

At the same time, you may look around and see many people who behave even worse than you do—they drink even more heavily, or they cheat more, or they hit their wives and girlfriends with their fists, or they are even more prone to bizarre outbursts; so you tell yourself, "how serious could my problem really be?"

Lastly, part of you may feel like life will be over if you accept having the issues she says you have.It might seem, for example- as if all of your enjoyment will disappear if you have to give up your destructive behaviors. From here on, life looks like drudgery and darkness.

- The substance abuser thinks; "how could life ever feel good if I can't drink and drug?"

- The person with mental health issues thinks; "how could life be exciting or satisfying without this wild roller-coaster ride of highs and lows that I live on?"

- The abusive man thinks; "how could I be a happy man if I have to allow my wife stand up to me and make decisions on equal terms?"

- The player may feel; "life is ruined if I can't keep several women going at a time."

The reality is that you will get a much more fulfilling life by turning yourself around.

Ask an alcoholic who has been sober for several years whether they miss their old partying days and he or she will usually say; "oh, yeah, I miss the drama and the fun sometimes, but I wouldn't want to go back to that for anything." They have discovered satisfaction on a deeper level.

Ask a reformed abuser whether he would like to get his old life back, and he'll say, "sure, there're times when I wish I could just shut my wife up the way I used to, but I wouldn't want to go back to seeing her so hurt, and to having my kids not trust me, and to feeling like such a jerk."

Ask someone who has overcome a personality disorder or a trauma history, and he or she will tell you, "I can find plenty of excitement in life without those wild swings I used to go through, and now I don't have to be living with a problem I'm trying to hide from everyone." Ask a man who finally grew up whether he wants to go back to being a thirty-three-year-old adolescent, and he'll say; "actually, it turns out the adult world isn't so bad."

So the rewards will come, though they won't come quickly. First you will have to do a lot of hard work, work that won't seem to pay off much in the short term- that's why so many men start making changes but then fail to carry them through. You will have to stop demanding instant gratification and stop insisting that the world owes you gratitude and rewards for doing what you should have been doing all along.

On the way—soon, in fact—you're going to need new friends. If you keep hanging out with your party pals you'll be back to partying very soon, and you'll keep convincing yourself that addictive behavior is normal since your friends all do the same things. If you keep spending your free time with men who speak contemptuously about women, you aren't going to break your own habits of looking down at females as second class. You won't get away from the land of denial if you're still surrounded by people who live there.

Homework:

Write a couple of paragraphs about what is scary or upsetting to you about admitting that you have a problem that has to be overcome. Then put down some of the reasons for believing that your partner is right (even if you aren't really ready to agree with her overall yet—just put the points that you do see down on paper). Third, put down a couple of thoughts about how you would enjoy your life more if you accepted the problem and changed the behavior. Last, go out for about a ten-minute walk by yourself, and let these thoughts and feelings roll around inside of you.

Lesson 7: Your First Steps Toward Change (Part 4):
Saying Goodbye To Payback

(Excerpted from L. Bancroft's Guide For Change (Part 1) (n.d.)

STEP THREE: saying good-bye to payback

Is revenge really as sweet as they say it is? Or is it actually a highly dysfunctional drive, one that keeps spreading more misery around the world and encourages people to find scapegoats for their own unhappiness?

In the context of intimate relationships, the answer is clear: the payback habit is a cancerous one, guaranteed to spread a deeper and deeper level of mistrust, resentment, and ultimately hatred into the connection between two people. It has to go.

If, for example, you deliberately make your partner feel bad because you're feeling bad, that absolutely will not "make her see what it's like," or "teach her a lesson," regardless of what you may tell yourself. She will learn only one thing: that she has to obey you and keep you happy, or you will hurt her.

Your relationship with her then stops being one between intimate partners, and becomes one between master and servant, between dominator and the dominated. Is this the impact you want to have on the world, to turn others into servants?

Even if you have only the narrowest, most self-serving goal of trying to make yourself feel better when you're upset, revenge still won't get you what you want. It brings only the most fleeting and superficial pleasure and like an addiction, leaves the person craving more rather than feeling satisfied.

As you may notice, payback-oriented people tend to be miserable anytime they aren't actively gloating — and that means most of the time they're miserable.

Here are some typical examples of retaliatory behavior:

- You and your partner are at a party and she complains that you are drinking too much, so you respond angrily by deliberately getting yourself completely (and embarrassingly) hammered.

- You are sick of your partner pressing you to carry your weight around the house, so you agree to do the dishes and then "accidentally" breaks two glasses, plus leave water spilled all over the kitchen floor, plus don't really get the dishes very clean, to make sure she won't ask you again.

- You are angry that she is confronting you about the demeaning way in which you speak to her, so you take off in the car and don't come back until after midnight, thereby causing her to worry about you and sticking her with all the work of getting the children ready for bed and tidying the house.

Do any of these behaviors sound familiar when you think back on how you've acted? These are all payback - pure and simple, and they have no place in the behavior of a mature and responsible person.

The alternative to payback is that you have to actually live with the uncomfortable feelings that are coming up for you in your conflicts with your partner. You also have to accept her right to disagree with you, to have her own thoughts and perceptions.

There are positive steps you can take to help you resist the temptation to punish her:

- Begin with deep, slow breaths, working on calming your heart rate and coming out of agitation.

- Self-impose a twenty-four-hour waiting period between the time that your partner does something that makes you angry and the time when you respond in words or actions; this will give you time to cool down and make sure that you makes choices that are not retaliatory.

- Each time you are very upset with her, you need to talk as soon as possible with someone who is a good influence on you; this person has to be someone who will settle you down rather than further fire you up against your partner, who will press you to think, and who will help you see the conflict through your partner's eyes.

- If you remain agitated, you should sit and write about what happened to help process your feelings. This writing should include some points that are positive about your partner's perspective even if you don't agree with her; you could write, for example, "I believe I'm doing my share with the kids, but I can also see why it wouldn't seem that way to her."

This process we are recommending leads us to the following central point in your work:

You will need, throughout the coming months and years, to be working all the time on improving your ability to take in, understand, and respect your partner's perspective on conflicts, including her ways of viewing you.

Homework:

Write descriptions of at least two incidents in which you were mad because you were sure that your partner was wrong about something, and it turned out that she was right. Next, write what is hard for you about giving up the payback habit. Last, write at least two examples of times you have gotten her back for things, and put some thoughts down about why your actions were harmful.

Lesson 8: Your First Steps Toward Change (Part 5): The Crucial Distinction Between Aggression And Self-Defense

(Excerpted from L. Bancroft's Guide For Change (Part 1) (n.d.)

The Crucial Distinction Between Aggression And Self-Defense

To make serious progress on your behavior, you will have to learn to make the absolutely critical separation between aggression (actions designed to harm the other person) and self-defense (actions designed to protect yourself). Destructive people get these two all wrapped up together, and tremendous harm follows. Specifically, you need to sort out clearly the difference between standing up for yourself and getting revenge. (See lists below.) It is simply unacceptable to use behaviors from the "Retaliation" list and then say, "I was just standing up for myself." You have to own the choices you've made in the past to use payback, and from here on out make different choices.

Standing Up For Yourself:

- Naming what you do not like; speaking angrily (but respectfully); explaining how her actions are making you feel.

- Taking time to yourself; pulling away briefly (but still meeting your responsibilities, not using the silent treatment, and not staying distant as a way to punish her).

- Asking for what you want her to do differently.

Retaliation:

- Saying things that are designed to hurt her feelings.

- Withdrawing in a way that sticks her with work to do, ruins plans, or uses the silent treatment.

- Not letting her talk.

- Getting intimidating or scary.

- Saying bad things about her to other people.

- Withdrawing your contribution to responsibilities.

- Trying to "make her feel" what you are feeling, trying to "do the same thing to her that she did to me"

- Collecting items off of the above list and accusing her that *she's* being retaliatory (which you would just be using as a way to retaliate against her, face it).

Trying to hurt the other person is *not* self-defense. Remember "two wrongs don't make a right"? Those ethics apply just as much to adults as to children.

Here's one way to summarize this section: from now on you have to choose something constructive that you can do with yourself when you are mad at her, instead of opting to do harm.

IMPORTANT NOTE: It's completely out of bounds to use any of this information against your partner. Don't start trying to catch her doing things on the "Retaliation" list, for example. That would be a sure sign that you want to stay stuck in your old habits.

STEP FOUR: making a plan for dealing with your issues

Deeply ingrained habits—meaning habits that a person has been acting out for years—carry a tremendous force that keeps them going. This force can seem as powerful and tenacious as a human being's will to live. Unless you make a clear plan for long-term change, you will never break your habits for very long; you will be stuck in a repeating pattern of:

- Apologies and promises to change.

- Next, a stage when your treatment of her gets a little better and you meet some of your responsibilities.

- And last, a stage where it all slides backward into your ruts of destructive living and blaming your partner for your own actions.

Now, you have probably promised her before — perhaps several times — that you would turn over a new leaf, and you probably meant it when you said it. So the promises, no matter how sincere they may be, just don't work. What has to be different now is that you will commit not only to what you are going to change, but also to *how* you are going to do it, with a written plan that you will share with your partner.

Your plan needs to include the specific elements listed below (which we will explain in detail):

The Elements Of Your Plan For Change

1. The specific behavioral changes you are going to make.

2. The specific destructive attitudes that you are going to let go of, and the constructive ones that will take their place.

3. The types of outside assistance you are going to get, including the specifics of how often you will go for help, how much of your past behavior you will truthfully reveal, how you will pay for services, and how much right your partner will have to know the details of what goes on in your work.

4. The types of day-to-day work you are going to do on your issues.

5. What you are committing to do if you break any element of your plan (this one is tricky, but it will make sense to you when we go over it).

6. How you will keep your partner informed about your work, which depends on how much she want to hear about it.

7. How you will get continued feedback from her about your actions and your progress, if she is open to giving it.

Let's look at a sample plan, and then we'll discuss each element and how it works. The numbers in the plan correspond to the numbered elements that we just described above.

Kelly's Plan

1. I will stop drinking and smoking weed. I will stop all secret communications with women I meet, and stop doing anything that implies to a woman that I'm interested in her or attracted to her. I will treat Renee like she's a valuable person and a high priority in my life all the time. I will commit myself fully to this relationship, and stop acting annoyed when Renee says we need to spend more time together and be more sexual.

2. I'm going to stop my self-talk about Renee being "too needy and too demanding," because what she is asking for is totally normal and is not that much. I'm going to focus on how the rewards of being in a close relationship outweigh the sacrifices. I'm going to remind myself that I'm responsible for my own actions.

   a. I will attend an AA meeting every day for the next three months. After that I will go to at least four meetings per week for a year, and then we'll discuss it again. I will get a sponsor by three weeks from now, which is February 15.

   b. I will reveal my problem with alcohol and weed to my parents and my siblings, and keep in touch with them about what I'm doing about it.

   c. I will talk to a counselor at my EAP program at work about the way I've used flirtations and affairs as a way to get back at Renee for complaining about my drinking and as a way to avoid committing to our relationship. I will make a plan with that counselor for staying away from those behaviors.

3. I will write in my journal every day about my temptations and about any self-talk that is negative about Renee or blames her for what a hard time I'm having. I will write for at least twenty minutes. However, I also will not use my AA meetings and journal writing as an excuse to not help with the cooking and cleaning or for not being sexually intimate with Renee (e.g., "I'm too busy, I'm too tired from my meeting, etc."). I will e-mail my sister at least twice a week about what is going on with me.

4. If I drink or drug again, I agree that I will go to an inpatient detox. If I have any flirtations or intimate contacts with women, I will move out of the house until Renee says I can come back, and not try to take any of the furniture or other stuff that belongs to both of us. If I skip any meetings or counseling appointments, I agree to move out for at least a month.

5. My journal is private, but Renee can read the e-mails between me and my sister if she wants to. (My sister agreed to this.) At least once a week I will tell Renee about what I'm learning in my meetings, and read her some sections aloud from my journal that I'm okay with sharing.

6. Renee does not want to have a regularly scheduled "feedback time" for now, but I agree to listen without interrupting whenever she has comments about my attitudes, my behavior, or how well I'm sticking to my plan. When this happens, I agree to give her a thoughtful, non-defensive response that day, or by the next morning at the latest.

This sample plan may give you enough of an idea about how to construct a plan, but here are some guidelines:

First, *you* make the plan; your partner doesn't make it for you, and you don't expect her to. Don't make a half-baked plan; put in a serious effort and cover all the bases, or don't do it at all.

Detailed, *specific* descriptions of behavioral and attitudinal changes are crucial. If you write vague goals such as "I'll be nicer to her," the plan won't help, because the side of you that wants to stay stuck (let's face it, that side is there) will keep insisting that you've been nice enough, and your behavior won't really change. Similarly such agreements as "I'll help around the house more," or "I'll keep a better attitude," or "I'll cut down on my drinking"will be unsuccessful. These need to be replaced with such statements as, "I will change at least four diapers a day and vacuum twice a week," "I won't snarl when you ask me to take care of something," and "I won't have more than two beers a week, and no other alcohol or weed."

The part where you agree to additional steps that you will take if you fall off your program is indispensable. The first reason is that if you've agreed ahead of time to accept specific consequences for breaking your plan, you lose some of the temptation to behave in unacceptable ways. Second, there is obviously a battle going on between two sides of your character, the side that wants to change and the side that wants to stay the same; and by committing ahead of time to respecting consequences, you can help the Good Side win.

Bear in mind that if you do break your plan, and then you *also* break your commitment about what you would do if you broke your plan, you will send your partner an unmistakable message that you don't plan to ever deal seriously with your issues. So it's worth it to stick by your word, even when it leads to hard times for you.

You don't want the old life anymore, so hang in there through the challenges of moving along the road to the new life.

Lesson 9: Your First Steps Toward Change (Part 6): Getting Proper Help

(Excerpted from L. Bancroft's Guide For Change (Part 1) (n.d.)

Getting Proper Help

Outside help is indispensable. It does not necessarily have to be professional help if you can't afford that, or if it isn't available to you. You might agree, for example, to speak three times a week with a friend or relative who you will not get sucked into your excuses and will hold you accountable.

If you have someone in your life who has recovered from addiction, or you know a person who insists on proper respectful treatment of others, or anyone else who cares about you enough to call you to order on your excuses and negative thinking, that person can be a resource for you.

You might also use self-help groups such as Alcoholics Anonymous or Smart Recovery.

If professional help is available, stop making excuses and use it. If you're saying you don't have the money to pay for counseling, but you do have money for beer and cigarettes, ball-game tickets, spiffier parts for your car, or new golf clubs, then the real issue is that you're afraid a counselor is going to see into you too well. But that's exactly why they might be able to help.

What Is The Right Kind Of Professional Help?

It has become popular in our society to tell one another, "you should go to therapy," as the solution to all personal problems. However, research on the effectiveness of counseling indicates that a successful outcome tends to come about only when the following conditions are met:

1. There is a particularly good fit between counselor and client;

2. There are clear goals set for the counseling process and a plan for how those goals will be achieved;

3. The type of counseling being used—and there are many different kinds—is appropriate for the client's personal style and the specific problems at hand.

4. Choosing a counselor or group therefore depends on what your primary problem is, using the following guidelines:

If your partner complains of abuse or mistreatment by you:

The appropriate service for a person who abuses his partner is called an "abuser intervention program" or a "batterer intervention program," where most of the work is done in groups. (In a few states, it is referred to as "batterer treatment," but that term has mostly gone out of use.) This is the right program for you even if you have never physically assaulted, sexually assaulted, or threatened her; in other words, even if your abuse does not include violence. If you say, "I'm not going to sit in a room with a bunch of batterers"—a common excuse used by abusive men to not attend a program—you're just making a new excuse.

If you abuse substances:

If you have a problem with alcohol or drugs, you will need to participate in a specialized substance abuse program. The options include:

1. Self-help groups such as Alcoholics Anonymous or Rational Recovery;

2. Outpatient substance abuse treatment, where you continue to stay at your home at night but get intensive group and/or individual counseling by day through a hospital, substance abuse clinic, or outpatient counseling service;

3. Programs where you stay at the facility for a period of time, known as "detoxes" or "in-patient substance abuse treatment."

These options can be thought of as levels of intervention, so that a person who does not manage to stop drinking through AA might need to try formal substance abuse treatment, and a person who fails in an outpatient program may need to go inpatient.

If you have mental health problems, including effects from trauma:

Most mental health counseling is known as "therapy" and is carried out by professionals known as "licensed clinicians." The most common forms are variations on "talk therapy," where the client sits in the therapist's office and discusses issues. Less common, but growing in popularity, are the "body-centered therapies," which still include some time spent talking but also involve elements of movement, massage, reexperiencing of deep emotions from the past, and other visceral experiences.

Some body-centered approaches, such as Sensorimotor Psychotherapy (which has been found to be especially effective for trauma survivors), do not involve any actual touching of the client by the therapist.

For people whose mental health problems appear to be rooted in traumatic experiences, such as child abuse, war, sexual assault, imprisonment, and countless other examples, there are the "trauma therapies"; these are new but promising approaches that are not widely available but worth looking for.

Finally, there are intensive programs that involve more than one meeting per week and a long-term commitment of as much as two years, the best-known (and most promising) one being "Dialectical Behavioral Therapy" or "DBT". DBT is commonly described as a treatment for Borderline Personality Disorder, but has promise as a therapy for anyone who has recurring patterns of behaving destructively toward themselves and of destroying close relationships.

DBT is also a good choice for you if:

1. You keep wishing your own behavior would improve but it doesn't, because you keep "losing it", or,

2. You keep feeling like the problem is actually that everyone around you is messed up and that you're fine, but your partner and/or other people are pointing out to you that you've got serious issues in your behavior and that your thinking is distorted.

Medical interventions are also present as an option, including psychiatric care and medication. Hospitalization in a psychiatric facility is available for severe mental health crises. Inform yourself carefully about psychiatric medication before using it; the long-term side effects can be much more serious than doctors will tell you (see *Anatomy Of An Epidemic* by Robert Whitaker).

If your partner is telling you that you are immature or selfish:

Specific services have not yet been designed for people who don't want to grow up, and who are reluctant to think about anyone other than themselves. So even though immaturity is not exactly a mental health problem, you will probably need to pursue a program for abusive people, for want of another option.

You might also try a therapist, to help you explore why you are still attached to having someone else look after you, and why you feel overwhelmed by the prospect of running your own life. Remember, though, to **keep the focus on action**; endless exploration of how you got that way can become another way to stay stuck.

"I Can Only Stand To Go To Counseling If She Comes With Me"

Going to counseling together with her is not going to help. **Meaningful change comes when you stop conditioning your behavior on what your partner does**, and agree to take responsibility for your own life and your own actions. If you go to counseling with her, you will keep bringing up what you feel she does wrong, which will leave you in the same rut you're in. It's time to stop using her as a crutch, or as a scratching post, and go do your own work.

I understand that you may feel that therapy is a mysterious and frightening process — many people feel this way — and so you want your partner to hold your hand through it.

But your first step is the most crucial one, and that's the step you take when you shoulder the responsibility to schedule your session and courageously take yourself off to it. The support you need will come from the therapist, not from your partner. It's time to stop blaming her, stop making her responsible and stop looking to her for things you should be doing for yourself.

Lesson 10: Your First Steps Toward Change (Part 7): Connecting to the Positive

(Excerpted from L. Bancroft's Guide For Change (Part 1) (n.d.)

STEP FIVE: Connecting yourself to the positive

What we think of as individual behavior is not really as "individual" as it seems. People look to one another for guidance on how to behave, and they tune in to approval or disapproval that they receive from their society and social network. Judgment is passed on our behavior at high levels—laws and police and courts—and at low levels, such as a friend frowning while we tell him or her about something we did.

Individuals who have chronically unhealthy behaviors appear not to care what society thinks of them, but if you look more closely, you find that they have at least a few people around them whose approval they are winning. This need for social acceptance is part of why drunks tend to hang out with other drunks and why men who abuse women tend to pick friends who are mistreating their own wives and girlfriends (as research has shown). Similarly, people who are chronic cheaters hang out with others who won't call them on their infidelity and will collude with them in keeping the secret from their partners.

So part of your growth process is to change the influences you are surrounding yourself with. First, you need to stop hanging out with, or even talking on the phone much with friends and relatives of yours who do any of the following:

- Avoid responsibility for their own actions, make lots of excuses themselves

- Laugh at your stories about your bad behavior, or are amused by your self-caused dramas

- Join with you in blaming your partner or in dismissing her feelings and concerns, back you up when you call to complain about her

- Have the same behavioral problems that you have

Look also at what kinds of messages you are getting from Internet sites you hang out on, books you read, and videos you watch. If you are into pornography, for example, you are absorbing a constant set of messages that support your disrespectful and immature attitudes. You can get a similar negative effect from websites that are made up of writings by men who blame women for all their problems and for everything that's wrong with the world.

So where can you look for people, and for values, that will push you toward growth instead of toward harm? You can:

- Make a point of spending more time talking to, or hanging out with men who have good relationships with their partners and don't speak badly about them

- Connect with female relatives of yours who are living lives that command respect

- Get more Involved with your church, temple, or other faith community—if it is a community that promotes respect and equality for women, and if it's a place where people see your issues rather than being fooled by the side of you that is in denial

- Find a mature, responsible sponsor in a twelve-step program

- Open yourself to more guidance and influence from your partner (but without leaning on her like a mother)

- Open yourself to more suggestions from her about people or groups you could be spending time around—and about which people to stay away from

In short, you need to unplug your brain from the values, attitudes, and excuses that you have been absorbing on a daily basis and choose an entirely new mental diet to nourish yourself with.

Add an item to your plan that addresses how you are going to surround yourself with more positive influences, and which people you need to be around less because they help you to stay stuck.

CAUTION: It's crucial to fight the temptation to flip these concepts around to use against your partner. For example, you could read what I wrote above and then turn it around, telling your partner that she should be more open to your influence about who *she* hangs around with. This is a dead end for multiple reasons:

1) You can't change if you're continuing to focus on her;

2) You need to accept that you have serious behavioral problems, and stop making it sound like that means your partner has those issues too;

3) Influence and control are two very different things; you need to stop *controlling her*, while also opening yourself for her to *influence you* more.

This is the conclusion of the section of lessons entitled, "Your First Steps Toward Change." Here's a recap of the beginning steps you need to make in order to change your life from being an abuser to being a healthy relationship partner:

1. Changing your attitude toward your partner's complaints;

2. Understanding your denial, and coming out of it;

3. Stopping your retaliations against your partner for raising grievances or for standing up for herself;

4. Making a plan;

5. Connecting to positive influences for growth and change.

These are all manageable steps, and the sooner you get down to business on taking them the less painful they will be. They are a crucial beginning to turning your life around. If you take the leap and make these straightforward efforts, you can bring yourself to the level where deep growth starts to occur.

Lesson 11: Setting Boundaries

What exactly are boundaries? Boundaries are decisions you make for yourself, not decisions you make for someone else. In order to set a boundary in a relationship, you can only control yourself. If someone else's behavior is destructive to you, then in order to set a boundary, the only thing you can do is ensure that you take care of yourself. For instance, if you have a loved one who uses drugs, you cannot make that person quit using drugs no matter what, it is purely their decision, but, what you can do is refuse to be around them while they are under the influence. The point to remember is you can only control yourself.

Another point to remember is that your boundaries belong to you. Other people cannot tell you what your boundaries should be. Each of us is unique and we each have a right to decide what we will or will not tolerate in our lives. In addition to this, sometimes we know what we need to do but we aren't ready to do it. We can only set boundaries when we're ready, not when someone else thinks we should.

The only way to make significant changes in your life in the area of boundaries is to set a clear, firm line in the sand, which is not blurred by compromises or a lack of resolve.

Here is an acronym from the word *Boundaries*, which describes what you need to do in order to take care of yourself when dealing with difficult or addictive personalities.

B = Belief System. The first step in setting boundaries is learning to challenge your old belief system, and begin a new way of thinking about yourself, others, God, and your situation. Remember, **our biggest captor is our own belief system**. Here is an example of a belief that you might want to challenge: "I can't kick him out, he'll be homeless." Perhaps a healthier belief is; "I will not live with an active alcoholic. If he chooses to keep drinking and ends up homeless, then that's his choice."

O = One Day at A Time. In order to overcome the fear of setting boundaries it is helpful to take baby steps and practice. Set your boundaries in small chunks. For instance, instead of completely refusing to see your difficult mother-in-law , give yourself a time limit. Tell yourself; "I'll only see her once a month for one hour. If she starts criticizing me then I'll leave earlier." This way you can practice setting "safe" boundaries for yourself, learning to take care of yourself one day at a time.

U = Understand yourself. You have probably been spending way too much time trying to understand the other person – the one whose behavior is driving you crazy. Instead of pouring all your energy into understanding why he does what he does, turn your energy inward and notice how you feel and learn why you spend so much time looking outward. Remember, **as long as you care more about your loved one's problem than he does, he won't have to**. Take your focus off the other person and place it on yourself, a place where you can actually effect change.

N = No is a complete sentence. You do not have to say yes to every request. In fact, only say yes to those requests that you genuinely want to undertake. Learn the art of saying, "No." Remember, practice makes perfect.

D = Develop yourself. Develop your boundary setting skills. Read about boundaries. Learn what experts and others have to say about how to develop your boundary-setting muscle. Practice one new thing every day to build your confidence. Remember, boundary setting is all about self-care. Develop the skill of self-care, through education, support groups, therapy, and practice.

A = Accept reality. Live in the truth. Do not continue to live in denial as you turn a blind eye to dysfunction. If someone is causing you harm, you need to look at the truth of the situation in order to set good boundaries.

R = Recovery. Boundaries are all about recovery. People who need to set boundaries must unlearn old, dysfunctional patterns of relating, and should be in a process of recovery, where they are recovering from these old, ineffective strategies.

I = Identifythe boundaries you want to set. Write them down. Think about what really matters in your life and how you can help yourself have a healthy lifestyle. Be honest with yourself and what you will and will no longer tolerate. It is okay to change your mind. If you have been "putting up" with something, it is okay to make the decision to stop putting up with it. Writing will help you sort these thoughts out.

E = Enough! Aren't you tired of this problem? Hasn't your enmeshment with it caused you more heartache than help? Tell yourself, "enough already!" Instead of giving your loved one a lecture, give yourself one. Tell yourself two things: "enough participation in this nonsense!" and "I am enough." You do not need theother person to change at all in order to have a good life. Tell yourself little pep talks all day long; reminding yourself of your value and worth and that you don't need this other person to change in order for you to have a fulfilling life.

S = Stop. Stop doing what you do to contribute to the problem. If you nag, lecture, point out, hint, react, cry, whine, fight, argue, manipulate, try to get others to help, or do anything else that involves trying to get someone else to change, stop. No longer use any of these strategies to get someone else to do or not do what you want. Change yourself. Walk away. Don't engage in insane behavior. Let it go and surrender. Remember, we all have a right to our choices. Focus on your own life and stop your part of the dysfunctional "dance." Give yourself permission to change.

Lesson 12: Different Types Of Anger

The following information was excerpted from, *Facing the Fire*, by John Lee.

As children, many of us feared anger because in our experience; it caused pain and abandonment. It hurt us because it was meant to hurt us. It was *unsafe anger*.

Perhaps one of your parents had rage or was passive aggressive. The purpose of this discussion is to help you learn to understand your personal relationship with anger and how to express it and process it in a healthy and non-abusive manner.

Types of Anger

Rage – The most obvious and shocking form of unsafe anger is rage. Rage explodes outward, into the world, and onto other people. Rage is uncontrollable and violent. When a person explodes with rage, oftentimes they "dump" it on others. Perhaps you have had this experience.

Rage is anger that has been buried and accumulating for years, often since childhood, that suddenly erupts when it is triggered by its resemblance to a present-day event or situation.

Passive Aggressive Anger- This type of anger is more subtle rage. It also goes out from an angry person into the world; but instead of exploding, it sneaks out. This is an unhealthy expression of anger.

Implosive Anger – This is anger directed inward. It is self-directed anger, and is very damaging. This, too, is an unhealthy expression of anger.

Present Anger -Present anger is caused by present events. It has an emotional force that is appropriate to its cause. Present anger can be expressed in either unhealthy or healthy ways.

Suppressed Anger – This is the type of anger that is left over from past events. Suppressed anger is misplaced into the present and is triggered by a present event.

Adult Suppressed Anger – This type of anger is caused by events that happened to us since we were adults; that is, since we have been more or less able to defend ourselves against other people.

Adult suppressed anger is a layer deeper than present anger because it has built up over time.

Cultural Suppressed Anger – This type of anger is harder to define than the other types of suppressed anger. This type of anger is caused by events that affect us because we are part of a certain culture (for example, being female.)

Infantile Suppressed Anger – This type of anger comes from traumatic events that happened to us during our first years of life; even prior to our ability to use language.

Though many of the incidents that caused us to feel angry or sad happened before we can consciously remember, the anger and grief they provoked are not forgotten, as the feelings are stored in our bodies. We "remember" this type of anger through our bodies.

Suppressed angers are cumulative, not exclusive

The three types of suppressed angers described above are not mutually exclusive. All three of these kinds of anger need to be released.

How to deal with your anger effectively

1. Understand what causes your anger
2. Get the anger out of your body

Remember:

- The body feels before the mind understands.
- Not only does the body feel before the mind understands, it also feels after.
- Understanding why anger is there does not make it go away.
- Until you get the emotional energy released from your body, you will be subject to your anger.

"Intellectually we never arrive; emotionally we arrive all the time." – Wallace Stevens

Lesson 13: Unhealthy Means of Expressing Anger

Because the anger so many of us experienced as children led to pain, we learned to protect ourselves in some ways. Many of us learned to find an escape route.

Running away was the course of protection for many. Unfortunately, that did not teach us how to have anger in a healthy and productive way. On the one hand, protecting oneself from another person's destructive anger is necessary; on the other hand, it really is not that effective.

Read the following unhealthy methods people use for escaping anger and see if any apply to you.

Shutting Down

In the earliest escape, our body, hurt or threatened with hurt, shuts down. This response is instinctive. This response protects us from feeling too much by numbing us out. The shutdown response is triggered by fear of hurt as well as by actual hurt. Most people come out of childhood reacting to anger by shutting down.

The Intellectual Escape

As very young children, perhaps as young as four or five years old, many of us learned to "control" our anger and protect ourselves from other people's anger by going intoour heads and either commanding our bodies to shut down or by rationalizing away the anger directed at us.

As adults this form of managing anger has been reinforced throughout the years by many institutions, including the church, school environments, etc. We have been taught that we can think our way through our anger. While this sounds good, the truth is – anger is felt in the body and thinking occurs in the head. You cannot think through a body experience.

When we intellectualize our anger, we are not expressing it; rather, we are repressing or suppressing it. We have "escaped" into our head. Many books reinforce this idea. Over and over again we are taught that we can deal with our anger by going into our heads and understanding it.

But, anger is not primarily an intellectual experience. While anger does have a mental component, it is mainly a bodily experience. It is *physical* energy. It is housed in the body as other emotional energies are. It is physical and visceral. It is not logical, rational, justifiable, or reasonable. It just is.

While the intellectual escape is advocated, by itself, it is ineffective for emotional health.

The Spiritual Escape

The spiritual escape, or spiritual *bypass*, is similar to the intellectual escape, except that religion replaces reason. You "bypass" your anger by praying, meditating, chanting, or focusing your attention on "higher" concepts.

Feelings are meant to be felt, not prayed away.

The Addiction Escape

Addictions are all about escaping emotions; this includes anger. Whether a person's addiction stimulates or depresses him, the addict does not release his emotions because he has not consciously confronted his feelings or dealt with his anger. Chemical addictions render the mind incompetent. Addictions deaden all emotions – those we want and those we don't want.

All Escapes Do the Same Thing

All of our escapes can deaden anger, but they don't get it out of our bodies. So rather than freeing us of our anger, they bind us to it.

Personal Reflection:

- Which type of method for expressing anger do you tend to use? How did you learn this method for expressing anger?

- What are your thoughts and feelings regarding anger? Are you comfortable expressing it?

- How do you feel around others who are expressing their anger?

Lesson 14: Coping With Anger (Part 1)

The following are a list of anger-release exercises as summarized by author John Lee, in his book, "*Facing the Fire*." It is important to learn how to express your anger in non-abusive and appropriate ways. These exercises will help you do just that.

Deep Breathing

Breathing helps you be in your body (the place where emotions reside) and also helps you heal. Whenever you feel emotionally threatened stop and focus on your breathing, taking deep, long, full-bodied breaths.

Breathing increases the energy in your body and allows that energy to move freely and be evenly distributed, so your brain or stomach isn't outrunning the rest of you.

Furthermore, if you're feeling something and you consciously keep breathing, you will be able to stay with that feeling until you've experienced it fully and it passes from you. If you stop or diminish your breathing, you will diminish the emotional experience.

Here's how to do it:

- Breathe in slowly, through your nose, until your stomach pushes out nearly as far as it will go.

- If you would like, place one hand on your chest and one hand on your stomach area. Make sure your stomach is rising, not your chest, to insure you are breathing properly.

- Breathe slowly, counting to 10.

- Pause before exhaling.

- Exhale slowly, through your mouth, counting to 10 as you do.

In summary, deep breathing:

1. Defends us against other people's feelings, while communicating to them that they are free to feel their feelings;

2. Increases our energy, to get us over the blues and the blahs;

3. Enables us to stay in our bodies and feel what we're feeling, however mild or strong these feelings are.

Breathing Exercise

To show you the healing power of deep breathing, let me suggest you find a comfortable place to sit where the light's not too bright. Loosen any tight clothing you are wearing, and begin breathing full, deep, slow, calm breaths. In and out. Close your eyes.

As you breathe, let any thoughts, pictures, or memories come up that want to. Let your mind roam. Don't only see what your mind brings to you, hear the sounds, smell the smells. Keep breathing.

After twenty breaths or so, you may begin feeling light-headed. This is normal. Don't worry about it. Continue breathing, slowly and calmly, and begin breathing a little less deeply.

Now, turn your mind to a time in your childhood when you were scared or anxious. Do not think of the worst memory you can come up with. Do not think of something terrible. Think of a time when you felt lonely and unsure. Recall the details of a particular incident. Where were you? Who were you with? What was the weather like? How did the air feel? What sounds did you hear? Keep breathing.

During this remembered event begin telling yourself to relax and breathe slowly, calmly, and deeply. Encourage your child-self until he or she is breathing in a relaxed manner. See your child-self become less scared and less rigid and less victimized. A part of you is that child. By simply thinking and breathing, you can heal that child in your mind.

Talking

It is both true and not true that talking through our feelings can heal us. Like breathing, talking is a fine way to express and release present anger. Talking can help express present anger, but it usually cannot handle deeply suppressed anger.

Talking about your anger – both present anger and suppressed anger - can be enormously helpful, provided you do it with a safe person. A safe person is someone who won't be hurt by what you have to say, and won't hurt you because you express anger.

It is helpful to talk to someone about your anger who is objective, healthy, safe, a good listener, and supportive. Keep in mind, though, that talking, alone, may not, in all cases, be enough to release the anger sufficiently. Releasing the anger using other methods may be necessary for some experiences of anger.

Talking Exercise

Think about the people in your life who are safe enough for you to "process" your feelings with. Who do you know that is safe, a good listener, compassionate, understanding, and mature enough to listen to you talk about anger without judgment or giving poor advice?

Now, think about something that you are angry about, what happened, how you felt, what your thoughts were.

Practice sharing your thoughts and feelings in a non-aggressive manner in the group if you feel it is safe to do so.

Lesson 15: Coping With Anger (Part 2): Writing

Lesson 16: Coping With Anger (Part 2): Writing

Lesson 17: Coping With Anger (Part 2): Writing

Lesson 18: Coping With Anger (Part 2): Writing

"This Chapter comprises a four week session. Group members will be required to think deeply through each assignment, complete homework, and bring back each week for discussion. This chapter is meant to be processed slowly in order for maximum benefit to occur."

Following are a list of anger-release exercises as summarized by author John Lee, in his book, "Facing the Fire." It is important to learn how to express your anger in non-abusive and appropriate ways. These exercises will help you do just that.

Note: These writing exercises are lengthy. This lesson will take three weeks to complete

Writing

Writing is like talking. It can release present and buried anger. It can lead to understanding anger of all levels, even the very deepest. You can do it alone.

Studies have shown that people who write about their most troubling experiences and inner most feelings may be healthier than those who don't. Autobiographical writing is healthy for two reasons:

1. It reduces physical and mental stress involved in inhibiting thoughts.

2. Writing helps to organize overwhelming events and make them manageable. Once organized, difficult thoughts are easier to resolve.

Writing Exercises

1. List of Dysfunctions

   Make a numbered list of all the dysfunctional things you do. Make the list as long as you can.

   Go back and concentrate on each item on the list, one by one. Feel what emotion each item causes you to feel. Write an M next to any item on your list that your mother did, and an F on any item on your list that your father did.

2. Sentence Completion.Complete the following Sentences:

When my dad got angry, he ..

When my mom got angry, she …

When I got angry as a child, I …

Which parent are you most like?

3. Description of your abandonment

Write about a time you were abandoned. Or, if you prefer, write about at time you were the saddest.

If you can, try doing this assignment with your non-dominant hand. Don't worry about the neatness of your writing. You're the only person who's going to see it. Breathe and relax as you write. Do not rush through this exercise.

4. List of people you're angry with

List every one you can think of that you're angry at, and also list the reasons for your anger. Go as far back in your memory as you can. No reason is unreasonable. No incident is too small. Do not evaluate your anger, simply describe   it.

This exercises helps you see what really matters to you. When you have made the list, add things to it as they come to mind.

Whatever you're angry about, respect that feeling enough to stay with it; let it work on you. You may be so moved that you need to express your emotion by screaming or beating a pillow or twisting a towel or doing a safe physical activity.

5. Letter writing

If it is possible for you to do so, write a letter using your non-dominant hand to someone you are really angry with. This could be your mother, your father, your spouse, your girlfriend or boyfriend, etc. It doesn't matter whether the person is living or dead because you are writing this letter for yourself, not for them. You are never going to give this letter to the person you are angry with.

In your letter, use whatever language comes out of you first. Be as vile, contemptuous, and blaming as you feel like. Tell the person you're writing to why you're so angry. Go into all the details. All of them – don't try to protect their feelings. Keep breathing.

6. Journal Keeping

Begin to keep a journal. Be truthful. Do not write in your journal the way you want to be; write in it how you really are.

It is very hard to get over one's need to appear good in other people's eyes. This same rule applies to journal writing. People do not even want to appear imperfect in their own private journals. In order for journaling to be effective, it is important to break through your mask and write your true, uncensored feelings when you journal.

Keep this in mind as you begin the habit of keeping a journal. Try to write every day in your journal. Write your true, honest feelings each day and see how you begin to heal from unexpressed anger.

Lesson 19: Emotional Intelligence

Written by: The Mind Tools editorial staff

Developing Strong "People Skills".

We probably all know people, either at work or in our personal lives, who are really good listeners. No matter what kind of situation we're in, they always seem to know just what to say – and how to say it – so that we're not offended or upset. They're caring and considerate, and even if we don't find a solution to our problem, we usually leave feeling more hopeful and optimistic.

Learn how to develop your emotional intelligence.

We probably also know people who are masters at managing their emotions. They don't get angry in stressful situations. Instead, they have the ability to look at a problem and calmly find a solution. They're excellent decision makers, and they know when to trust their intuition. Regardless of their strengths, however, they're usually willing to look at themselves honestly. They take criticism well, and they know when to use it to improve their performance.

People like this have a high degree of emotional intelligence. They know themselves very well, and they're also able to sense the emotional needs of others.

Would you like to be more like this?

As more and more people accept that emotional intelligence is just as important to professional success as technical ability, organizations are increasingly using it when they hire and promote.

For example, one large cosmetics company recently revised their hiring process for salespeople to choose candidates based on their emotional intelligence. The result? People hired with the new system have sold, on average, $91,000 more than salespeople selected under the old system. There has also been significantly lower staff turnover among the group chosen for their emotional intelligence.

So, what exactly is emotional intelligence, and what can you do to improve yours?

What Is Emotional Intelligence?

We all have different personalities, different wants and needs, and different ways of showing our emotions. Navigating through this all takes tact and cleverness – especially if we hope to succeed in life. This is where emotional intelligence becomes important.

Emotional intelligence is the ability to recognize your emotions, understand what they're telling you, and realize how your emotions affect people around you. It also involves your perception of others: when you understand how they feel, this allows you to manage relationships more effectively.

People with high emotional intelligence are usually successful in most things they do. Why? Because they're the ones that others want on their team. When people with high emotional intelligence send an email, it gets answered. When they need help, they get it. Because they make others feel good, they go through life much more easily than people who are easily angered or upset.

Characteristics of Emotional Intelligence

In his book titled "Emotional Intelligence - Why It Can Matter More Than IQ,1995", Daniel Goleman, an American psychologist, developed a framework of five elements that define emotional intelligence:

Self-Awareness – People with high emotional intelligence are usually very self-aware. They understand their emotions, and because of this, they don't let their feelings rule them. They're confident – because they trust their intuition and don't let their emotions get out of control.

They're also willing to take an honest look at themselves. They know their strengths and weaknesses, and they work on these areas so they can perform better. Many people believe that this self-awareness is the most important part of emotional intelligence.

Self-Regulation – This is the ability to control emotions and impulses. People who self-regulate typically don't allow themselves to become too angry or jealous, and they don't make impulsive, careless decisions. They think before they act. Characteristics of self-regulation are thoughtfulness, comfort with change, integrity, and the ability to say no.

Motivation – People with a high degree of emotional intelligence are usually motivated. They're willing to defer immediate results for long-term success. They're highly productive, love a challenge, and are very effective in whatever they do.

Empathy – This is perhaps the second-most important element of emotional intelligence. Empathy is the ability to identify with and understand the wants, needs, and viewpoints of those around you. People with empathy are good at recognizing the feelings of others, even when those feelings may not be obvious. As a result, empathetic people are usually excellent at managing relationships, listening, and relating to others. They avoid stereotyping and judging too quickly, and they live their lives in a very open, honest way.

Social Skills – It's usually easy to talk to and like people with good social skills - another sign of high emotional intelligence. Those with strong social skills are typically team players. Rather than focus on their own success first, they help others develop and shine. They can manage disputes, are excellent communicators, and are masters at building and maintaining relationships.

As you've probably determined, emotional intelligence can be a key to success in your life – especially in your career. The ability to manage people and relationships is very important in all leaders, so developing and using your emotional intelligence can be a good way to show others the leader inside of you.

How To Improve Your Emotional Intelligence

The good news is that emotional intelligence can be learned and developed. As well as working on your skills in the five areas above, use these strategies:

Observe how you react to people. Do you rush to judgment before you know all of the facts? Do you stereotype? Look honestly at how you think and interact with other people. Try to put yourself in their place, and be more open and accepting of their perspectives and needs.

Look at your work environment. Do you seek attention for your accomplishments? Humility can be a wonderful quality, and it doesn't mean that you're shy or lack self-confidence. When you practice humility, you say that you know what you did, and you can be quietly confident about it. Give others a chance to shine – put the focus on them, and don't worry too much about getting praise for yourself.

Do a self-evaluation. What are your weaknesses? Are you willing to accept that you're not perfect and that you could work on some areas to make yourself a better person? Have the courage to look at yourself honestly – it can change your life.

Examine how you react to stressful situations. Do you become upset every time there's a delay or something doesn't happen the way you want? Do you blame others or become angry at them, even when it's not their fault? The ability to stay calm and in control in difficult situations is highly valued – in the business world and outside it. Keep your emotions under control when things go wrong.

Take responsibility for your actions. If you hurt someone's feelings, apologize directly – don't ignore what you did or avoid the person. People are usually more willing to forgive and forget if you make an honest attempt to make things right.

Examine how your actions will affect others – before you take those actions. If your decision will impact others, put yourself in their place. How will they feel if you do this? Would you want that experience? If you must take the action, how can you help others deal with the effects?

Emotional Intelligence Homework Assignment

For your homework assignment this week, please take the following quiz.

Emotional Intelligence Test

(Source: Paul Mohapel, San Diego City College MESA Program)

Emotional intelligence is your ability to be aware of, understand, and manage your emoitons. Why is emotional intelligence important? While intelligence is important, success in life depends more on emotional intelligence. Take this assessment to learn your EQ strengths.

Scoring: Rank each statement as follows: 0 – Never; 1-Rarely; 2-Sometimes; 3-Often; 4-Always

Emotional Awareness:

0 1 2 3 4	My feelings are clear to me at any given moment.
0 1 2 3 4	Emotions play an important part in my life.
0 1 2 3 4	My moods impact the people around me.
0 1 2 3 4	I find it easy to put words to my feelings.
0 1 2 3 4	My moods are easily affected by external events.
0 1 2 3 4	I can easily sense when I'm going to be angry.
0 1 2 3 4	I readily tell others my true feelings.
0 1 2 3 4	I find it easy to describe my feelings.
0 1 2 3 4	Even when I'm upset, I'm aware of what's happening to me.
0 1 2 3 4	I am able to stand apart from my thoughts and feelings and examine them.

Emotional Awareness – Total: _____

Emotional Management:

0 1 2 3 4	I accept responsibility for my actions.
0 1 2 3 4	I find it easy to make goals and stick with them.
0 1 2 3 4	I am an emotionally balanced person.
0 1 2 3 4	I am a very patient person.
0 1 2 3 4	I can accept critical comments from others without becoming angry.
0 1 2 3 4	I maintain my composure, even during stressful times.
0 1 2 3 4	If an issue does not affect me directly, I don't let it bother me.
0 1 2 3 4	I can restrain myself when I feel anger towards someone.
0 1 2 3 4	I control urges to overindulge in things that could damage my well being.
0 1 2 3 4	I direct my energy into creative work or hobbies.

Emotional Management – Total: _____

Social Emotional Awareness:

0 1 2 3 4	I consider the impact of my decisions on other people.

0 1 2 3 4	I can easily tell if the people around me are becoming annoyed.
0 1 2 3 4	I sense it when a person's mood changes.
0 1 2 3 4	I am able to be supportive when giving bad news to others.
0 1 2 3 4	I am generally able to understand the way other people feel.
0 1 2 3 4	My friends can tell me intimate things about themselves.
0 1 2 3 4	It genuinely bothers me to see other people suffer.
0 1 2 3 4	I usually know when to speak and when to be silent.
0 1 2 3 4	I care what happens to other people.
0 1 2 3 4	I understand when people's plans change.

Social Emotional Awareness – Total: _____

Relationship Management:

0 1 2 3 4	I am able to show affection.
0 1 2 3 4	My relationships are safe places for me.
0 1 2 3 4	I find it easy to share my deep feelings with others.
0 1 2 3 4	I am good at motivating others.
0 1 2 3 4	I am a fairly cheerful person.
0 1 2 3 4	It is easy for me to make friends.
0 1 2 3 4	People tell me I am sociable and fun.
0 1 2 3 4	I like helping people.
0 1 2 3 4	Others can depend on me.
0 1 2 3 4	I am able to talk someone down if they are very upset.

Relationship Management – Total: _____

DOMAIN	SCORE
Emotional Awareness	0 2 4 6 8 10 12 14 16 18 20 22 24 26 28 30 32 34 36 38 40
Emotional Management	0 2 4 6 8 10 12 14 16 18 20 22 24 26 28 30 32 34 36 38 40
Social Emotional Awareness	0 2 4 6 8 10 12 14 16 18 20 22 24 26 28 30 32 34 36 38 40
Relationship Management	0 2 4 6 8 10 12 14 16 18 20 22 24 26 28 30 32 34 36 38 40

Measure your effectiveness in each domain using the following key:

0 – 24	Area for Enrichment: Requires attention and development.
25 - 34	Effective Functioning: Consider strengthening
35 – 40	Enhanced Skills: Use as leverage to develop weaker areas

Using your EQ strength – For your strongest EQ domain, give an example of how you demonstrate your strength in your daily life or work:

Effects of your EQ strength – For your weakest EQ domain, give an example of how this affects you and other in your daily life.

Improving your EQ strength – For your weakest EQ domain, what steps can you take to strengthen yourself in this area? How will this benefit you in your daily life?

Lesson 20: Healthy Communication

"Life is a series of moments, all present." – John Lee

Listening

Written by Caleb Storkey

Here are 11 steps to improve your listening skills.

1. A good listener is attentive. They make good eye contact, don't interrupt what the other person is saying and show an interest in what is being communicated. There's always something incredible you can hear in anyone's story.

2. A good listener does not look over the shoulder of the person that's speaking, waiting for someone more interesting to come along.

3. A good listener does not check their phone or tablet in the middle of a conversation, when someone is sharing with them.

4. A good listener is not waiting for their chance to get a word in, treating the 'period of listening' as a pause in their 'monologue.' Being so focused on trying to get one's view over is insensitive and misses the real value in the conversation.

5. A good listener uses positive body language; leaning forward and showing an enthusiastic, relaxed nature. They don't fidget, cross arms, look elsewhere or express inappropriate shock or disbelief at whatis shared.

6. A good listener does not hurry another person, but asks good questions to guide the sharing. They guide and help shape what's being shared, but if the other person feels cut off or squashed they've failed.

7. A good listener does not approach a conversation with prejudice, expecting to know what's going to come out of the speaker's lips. They don't listen with a pre-formed opinion but attempt to have an open mind to what's being communicated. It's amazing how much time is wasted with the belief that people understand what someone else means without taking the effort and time to listen.

8. A good listener cares. They show empathy for what the other person has to say. It's genuine, authentic and comes from a place of truthful concern.

9. A good listener identifies areas of agreement with the speaker whilst avoiding the cliché statement: "I know exactly how you feel." Because you don't. It ends up sounding insensitive, trite or self-centered. Everyone loves to be truly understood. No one likes to be patronized.

10. A good listener remembers. They remember and follow up conversations wherever possible. They treat what is shared with respect and where appropriate contribute in ongoing interaction.

11. A good listener knows how to treat what is shared with confidentiality. They are trustworthy and sensitive with information and never look to use anything that is shared for any purpose other than good.

Assertive and Respectful Communication

Adapted from Vivian Barnette

Assertiveness is the ability to honestly express your opinions, feelings, attitudes,and rights in a way that respects the rights of others.Many of us are taught that we should always concede or defer to others. We learnthat it is selfish to consider our needs above those of others and if someone doessomething we don't like, we should just be quiet and stay away from that person inthe future.

However, assertive communication is important because it helps usavoid:

- Resentment. Anger at others for manipulating or taking advantage of me.

- Frustration. How could I be such a wimp? Why did I let them walk all over me?

- Anxiety and Avoidance. If you begin to avoid situations or people that you know will make you uncomfortable, you may miss out on fun activities, job opportunities, relationships, and lots of other good stuff.

When planning your assertive behavior, remember that the other person is used toyou behaving in a certain way and may be confused when you change yourcommunication style. Tell the other person up front what you're trying to do.

Choose a peaceful moment for this.

Assertive communication with others has three important components:

1. **Empathy/validation**: Try to say something that shows your understanding of theother person's feelings. This shows the other person that you're not trying to picka fight and it takes the wind out of their sails.

   For example:"I know that you get anxious when you're ready to go and I'm not …"

2. **Statement of problem:** This piece describes your difficulty or dissatisfactionwith the situation and tells why you need something to change.

For example:"… but when you do that, I get all flustered and take even more time.By the time we get in the car, we're mad at each other and not muchin the mood to have a good time."

3. **Statement of what you want**: This is a specific request for a specific change inthe other person's behavior.

   For example: "From now on, let's be sure we know what time we want to leave, andif you're ready before I am, will you please just go to another roomand read the paper or watch TV?"

How to be effectively assertive:

- **Use assertive body language.** Face the other person, stand or sit straight,don't use dismissive gestures, be sure you have a pleasant, but serious, facialexpression, keep your voice calm and soft, not whiney or abrasive.

- **Use "I" statements.** Focus on the problem you're having, not on accusing orblaming the other person. Example: "I'd like to tell my stories withoutinterruption." instead of "You're always interrupting my stories!"

- **Use facts, not judgments**. Example: "Your punctuation needs work and yourformatting is inconsistent" instead of "This is sloppy work." or "Do youknow that shirt has some spots?" instead of "You're not going out lookinglike THAT, are you?"

- **Express ownership of your thoughts, feelings, and opinions**. Example: "I getangry when he breaks his promises." instead of "He makes me angry." or "Ibelieve the best policy is to…" instead of "The only sensible thing is to …"

- **Make clear, direct requests**. Don't invite the person to say, "No." Example: "Will you please…?" instead of, "Would you mind…?"

Lesson 21: Understanding Cognitive Distortions

The following information was written by J. M. Grohol, Psy D.

What is a cognitive distortion and why do so many people have them? Cognitive distortions are simply ways that our mind convinces us of something that isn't really true. These inaccurate thoughts are usually used to reinforce negative thinking or emotions — telling ourselves things that sound rational and accurate, but really only serve to keep us feeling bad about ourselves.

For instance, a person might tell themselves, "I always fail when I try to do something new; I therefore fail at everything I try." This is an example of "black or white" (or polarized) thinking. The person is only seeing things in absolutes — that if they fail at one thing, they must fail at all things. If they added, "I must be a complete loser and failure" to their thinking, that would also be an example of overgeneralization — taking a failure at one specific task and generalizing it their very self and identity.

Cognitive distortions are at the core of many cognitive behavioral problemsand other kinds of problem that therapists help a person learn to change in psychotherapy. By learning to correctly identify this kind of "stinkin' thinkin'," a person can then answer the negative thinking back, and refute it. By refuting the negative thinking over and over again, it will slowly diminish overtime and be automatically replaced by more rational, balanced thinking.

Cognitive Distortions

Aaron Beck first proposed the theory behind cognitive distortions and David Burns was responsible for popularizing it with common names and examples for the distortions.

1. Filtering

We take the negative details and magnify them while filtering out all positive aspects of a situation. For instance, a person may pick out a single, unpleasant detail and dwell on it exclusively so that their vision of reality becomes darkened or distorted.

2. Polarized Thinking (or "Black and White" Thinking)

In polarized thinking, things are either "black-or-white." We have to be perfect or we're a failure — there is no middle ground. You place people or situations in "either/or" categories, with no shades of gray or allowing for the complexity of most people and situations. If your performance falls short of perfect, you see yourself as a total failure.

3. Overgeneralization

In this cognitive distortion, we come to a general conclusion based on a single incident or a single piece of evidence. If something bad happens only once, we expect it to happen over and over again. A person may see a single, unpleasant event as part of a never-ending pattern of defeat.

4. Jumping to Conclusions

Without individuals saying so, we know what they are feeling and why they act the way they do. In particular, we are able to determine how people are feeling toward us.

For example, a person may conclude that someone is reacting negatively toward them but doesn't actually bother to find out if they are correct. Another example is a person may anticipate that things will turn out badly, and will feel convinced that their prediction is already an established fact.

5. Catastrophizing

We expect disaster to strike, no matter what. This is also referred to as "magnifying or minimizing." We hear about a problem and use *what if* questions (e.g., "What if tragedy strikes?" "What if it happens to me?").
For example, a person might exaggerate the importance of insignificant events (such as their mistake, or someone else's achievement). Or they may inappropriately shrink the magnitude of significant events until they appear tiny (for example, a person's own desirable qualities or someone else's imperfections).

6. Personalization

Personalization is a distortion where a person believes that everything others do or say is some kind of direct, personal reaction to the person. We also compare ourselves to others trying to determine who is smarter, better looking etc.

A person engaging in personalization may also see themselves as the cause of some unhealthy external event that they were not responsible for. For example, "We were late to the dinner party and *caused* the hostess to overcook the meal. If I had only pushed my husband to leave on time, this wouldn't have happened."

7. Control Fallacies

If we feel *externally controlled*, we see ourselves as helpless a victim of fate. For example, "I can't help it if the quality of the work is poor; my boss demanded I work overtime on it." The fallacy of *internal control* has us assuming responsibility for the pain and happiness of everyone around us. For example, "Why aren't you happy? Is it because of something I did?"

8. Fallacy of Fairness

We feel resentful because we think we know what is fair, but other people won't agree with us. As our parents tell us when we're growing up and something doesn't go our way, "Life isn't always fair." People who go through life applying a measuring ruler against every situation judging its "fairness" will often feel badly and negative because of it. Because life isn't "fair" — things will not always work out in your favor, even when you think they should.

9. Blaming

We hold other people responsible for our pain, or take the other track and blame ourselves for every problem. For example, "stop making me feel bad about myself!" Nobody can "make" us feel any particular way — only we have control over our own emotions and emotional reactions.

10. Shoulds

We have a list of ironclad rules about how others and we should behave. People who break the rules make us angry, and we feel guilty when we violate these rules. A person may often believe they are trying to motivate themselves with "shoulds" and "should nots", as if they have to be punished before they can do anything.

For example, "I really should exercise. I shouldn't be so lazy. "Musts and oughts" are also offenders. The emotional consequence is guilt. When a person directs "should statements" towards others, they often feel anger, frustration and resentment.

11. Emotional Reasoning

We believe that what we feel must be true automatically. If we feel stupid and boring, then we must be stupid and boring. You assume that your unhealthy emotions reflect the way things really are — "I feel it, therefore it must be true."

12. Fallacy of Change

We expect that other people will change to suit us if we just pressure or cajole them enough. We need to change people because our hopes for happiness seem to depend entirely on them.

13. Global Labeling

We generalize one or two qualities into a negative global judgment. These are extreme forms of generalizing, and are also referred to as "labeling" and "mislabeling." Instead of describing an error in context of a specific situation, a person will attach an unhealthy label to themselves.

For example, they may say, "I'm a loser" in a situation where they failed at a specific task. When someone else's behavior rubs a person the wrong way, they may attach an unhealthy label to him, such as "He's a real jerk." Mislabeling involves describing an event with language that is highly colored and emotionally loaded. For example, instead of saying someone drops her children off at daycare every day, a person who is mislabeling might say that "she abandons her children to strangers."

14. Always Being Right

We are continually on trial to prove that our opinions and actions are correct. Being wrong is unthinkable and we will go to any length to demonstrate our rightness. For example, "I don't care how badly arguing with me makes you feel, I'm going to win this argument no matter what, because I'm right." Being right often is more important than the feelings of others around a person who engages in this cognitive distortion, even loved ones.

15. Heaven's Reward Fallacy

We expect our sacrifice and self-denial to pay off, as if someone is keeping score. We feel bitter when the reward doesn't come.

Lesson 22: Fixing Cognitive Distortions

The following information was written by J. M. Grohol, Psy D.

Cognitive distortions have a way of playing havoc with our lives. If we let them. This kind of "stinkin' thinkin'" can be "undone," but it takes effort and lots of practice — every day. If you want to stop the irrational thinking, you can start by trying out the exercises below.

1. Identify Your Cognitive Distortions

It helps to create a list of our troublesome thoughts and examine them later for matches with a list of cognitive distortions. An examination of your cognitive distortions allows you to see which distortions you prefer. Additionally, this process will allow you to think about your problem or predicament in more natural and realistic ways.

2. Examine The Evidence

A thorough examination of an experience will help you to identify the basis for your distorted thoughts. If you are quite self-critical, then, it would benefit you to greatly identify a number of experiences and situations where you had success.

3. Double Standard Method

An alternative to "self-talk" that is harsh and demeaning is to talk to yourself in the same compassionate and caring way that you would talk with a friend in a similar situation.

4. Thinking In Shades of Gray

Instead of thinking about your problem or predicament in an "either-or" polarity, evaluate things on a scale of 0-100. When a plan or goal is not fully realized, think about and evaluate the experience as a partial success, again, on a scale of 0-100.

5. Survey Method

It helps to seek the opinions of others regarding whether your thoughts and attitudes are realistic. If you believe that your anxiety about an upcoming event is unwarranted, check with a few trusted friends or relatives.

6. Definitions

What does it mean to define yourself as "inferior," "a loser," "a fool," or "abnormal." An examination of these and other global labels likely will reveal that they more closely represent specific behaviors, or an identifiable behavior pattern instead of the total person.

Examine labels you have placed on others as well as yourself. Learn to see where you are using name-calling and labeling as methods for thinking in terms of all or nothing definitions.

7. Re-attribution

Often, people automatically blame themselves or others for the problems and predicaments they experience. To help with the "blame game" learn to identify external factors and that contributed to the problem.

Regardless of the degree of responsibility you assign to a problem, your energy is best utilized in the pursuit of resolutions to problems or identifying ways to cope with predicaments, rather than assigning blame.

8. Cost-Benefit Analysis

It is helpful to list the advantages and disadvantages of feelings, thoughts, or behaviors. A cost-benefit analysis will help us to ascertain what you are gaining from feeling bad, distorted thinking, and inappropriate behavior.

Exercise

List the cognitive distortions you use in your life. Write the costs and benefits of each. Share with your group.

Lesson 23: Cultural And Social Norms That Support Violence

(By: the World Health Organization)

Cultural and social norms that support violence including sexual violence, as a private affair hinders outside intervention and prevents those affected from speaking out and gaining support.In many societies, victims of sexual violence also feel stigmatized, which inhibits reporting.

Additionally, strong evidence of an association between alcohol consumption and violent behavior means that cultural and social norms around alcohol use and its expected effects can also encourage and justify violent acts. In a number of countries, harmful alcohol use is estimated to be responsible for 26% of male and 16% of female disability-adjusted life-years lost as a result of homicide.

Societies that tolerate higher rates of acute alcohol intoxication report stronger relationships between alcohol use and violence than those where drinking occurs more moderately. Furthermore, alcohol-related violence is considered more likely in cultures where many believe that alcohol plays a positive role by helping people to shed their inhibitions. Here, alcohol can be used as a justification for violent behavior, or consumed to fuel the courage needed to commit violent crimes.

Interventions that tackle the cultural and social norms underlying risky drinking behavior can help in preventing violence.

A variety of external and internal pressures are thought to maintain cultural and social norms. Thus, individuals are discouraged from violating norms by the threat of social disapproval or punishment and feelings of guilt and shame that result from the internalization of norms.

Cultural and social norms do not necessarily correspond with an individual's attitudes (positive or negative feelings towards an object or idea) and beliefs (perceptions that certain premises are true),although they may influence these attitudes and beliefs, if norms becomes internalized.

Cultural and social norms also vary widely; so, behavior acceptable o one social group, gang or culture may not be tolerated in another.

Different cultural and social norms support different types of violence. For instance, traditional beliefs that men have a right to control or discipline women through physical means makes women vulnerable to violence by intimate partners and places girls at risk of sexual abuse. Equally, cultural acceptance of violence encourages the risk of violence within family relationships.

Cultural and social norms supporting different types of violence

Child maltreatment

- Female children are valued less in society than males (e.g. Peru, where female children are considered to have less social and economic potential).
- Children have a low status in society and within the family (e.g. Guatemala).
- Physical punishment is an acceptable or normal part of rearing a child (e.g. Turkey, Ethiopia.)
- Communities adhere to harmful traditional cultural practices such as genital mutilation (e.g. Nigeria, Sudan) or child marriage.

Intimate partner violence

- A man has a right to assert power over a woman and is socially superior (e.g. India, Nigeria, Ghana,China).
- A woman's freedom should be restricted (e.g. Pakistan).
- A man has a right to "correct" or discipline female behavior.
- Physical violence is an acceptable way to resolve conflicts within a relationship (e.g. South Africa,China).
- A woman is responsible for making a marriage work (e.g. Israel).
- Intimate partner violence is a taboo subject (e.g. South Africa) and reporting abuse is disrespectful(Nigeria).
- Divorce is shameful (e.g. Pakistan).
- When a dowry (financial payment from the bride's family to the husband) or bride wealth (financial payment from the husband to the bride's family) is an expected part of marriage (e.g. Nigeria, India), violence can occur either because financial demands are not met, or because bride wealth becomes synonymous with purchasing and thus owning a wife.
- A man's honor is linked to a woman's sexual behavior. Here, any deviation from sexual norms disgraces the entire family, which can then lead to honor killings (e.g. Jordan).

Suicide and self-harm

- Mental health problems are embarrassing and shameful, deterring individuals from seeking help (e.g. Australia, Brazil).
- Individuals in different social groups within society are not tolerated – e.g. homosexuals (Japan).

Sexual violence

- Sex is a man's right in marriage (e.g. Pakistan)
- Girls are responsible for controlling a man's sexual urges (e.g. South Africa).

- Sexual violence is an acceptable way of putting women in their place or punishing them (e.g. South Africa).
- Sexual activity (including rape) is a marker of masculinity (e.g. South Africa).
- Sex and sexuality are taboo subjects (e.g. Pakistan).

Youth violence

- Cultural intolerance, intense dislike and stereotyping of "different" groups within society (e.g. (e.g. xenophobic or racist violence and homophobic violence).

Community violence

- Reporting youth violence or bullying is unacceptable (e.g. the United Kingdom).
- Sexual violence such as rape is shameful for the victim, which prevents disclosure (e.g. the United States)

Homework Assignment:

How have cultural norms affected your personal view of how to be in a family/relationship?

What have you learned from your family with regards to how to treat others and how to be treated?

How have other social groups, such as neighborhoods, gangs, or other affiliations that you associate with influenced your beliefs and behaviors towards how to treat an intimate partner?

Lesson 24: Family History Exercise

One important part of recovering from destructive behaviors is to examine your own childhood and how your family history has played a role in your development. The following questions can help you study your family history to see if there have been any circumstances of abuse or trauma in your background.

- Who lived in your house growing up? How many siblings did you have? What was your birth order?

- List three words to describe your relationship with your father as a child and describe one experience that indicates why you chose these particular words.

- List three words to describe your relationship with your mother as a child and describe one experience that indicates why you chose these particular words.

- How was your family dysfunctional (if at all?) Is there addiction, mental illness, physical illness, poverty, sexual abuse, domestic violence, or something else, or a combination of these things?

- Were your parents able to assume most of the normal parental duties? If not, did they get done? If so, who did them? If not, how did that affect you?

- Did odd things happen that you began to see as normal? If so, what?

- Were you afraid to have friends over? Did your parent(s) ever embarrass, scare, or anger you?

- Did family members walk on eggshells to try to avoid an explosion? If so, why did this happen?

- How did your family demonstrate love when you were growing up? How did they demonstrate anger?

- What did your father teach you about manhood?

- What did your mother teach you about womanhood?

- Was there any type of abuse happening in your home as a child? If so, how did this impact you?

- Please describe any other significant events that happened in your childhood that significantly affected your life.

Lesson 25: Repeating Unhealthy Patterns

Written By Mary Darling Montero, LCSW

Have you ever felt that certain patterns keep popping up in your relationships with significant others, family, friends, bosses or coworkers and wondered why? After a relationship breakup or divorce is an ideal time to explore this. Most of us, often without realizing it, follow distinct patterns in our relationships—patterns that may be ingrained in our personalities. It's unrealistic, of course, to aspire to a complete personality overhaul, but what we can do is examine old patterns, learn to be aware of how they're affecting our relationships and begin to alter them.

When a person comes to me for therapy after a breakup or divorce, especially if the relationship was challenging, one of my tasks is to explore the dynamics of not only the relationship in question, but all other significant relationships in the person's life as well—all the way back to parents or other primary caregivers. The dynamics of those relationships offer clues as to why we repeat the same behaviors again and again in our interactions with others.

The widespread belief is that these patterns are largely unconscious, operating in areas of our brains that are not always connected to our awareness. Just as breathing and walking do not require us to think, many of our interactions with and reactions to others happen automatically. The notion that interactions with our primary caregivers throughout our childhoods determine unconscious patterns of security, trust and independence that we carry into adulthood is not new.

Relatively recently, the field of neuroscience exploded with findings about how the brain works, much of which backs up the notion that significant relationships and experiences in our lives can imprint unconscious memories in our brains—memories that can be triggered later in life and lead to certain feelings and behaviors without us even realizing what's going on.

The idea of history repeating itself can be looked at in two ways: patterns that remain constant throughout our lives, and an isolated incident that brings about unexpected feelings or behaviors, seemingly out of the blue.

Take "Jaclyn" for example, a client who came to therapy and discovered that in all of her romantic, professional, social and familial relationships she tended to put her own needs on the back burner. In other words, she was a "people pleaser." As a result, her own needs were not being met on a consistent basis. Her romantic relationships were unhealthy and her sense of self was wavering. She traced this pattern back to her childhood, when her parents were going through a divorce and she felt neglected. The only way she felt she could gain her parents' attention and approval was by pleasing them, and by not rocking the boat in any way. She carried this pattern into adulthood and was finally able to learn that asserting herself in healthy ways didn't push people away. In fact, it made for better relationships and a more secure sense of self.

In the case of isolated incidents, consider "Paul." After his wife received a promotion and began to work longer hours (becoming less physically and emotionally available) Paul found himself acting in ways that were out of character. He began to pull away from his wife. He sat in silence and pouted. He became passive-aggressive, responding to his wife with sarcasm and what he described as "dirty looks."

Paul felt baffled by his behavior. He said, "I've never acted like this in my life!" In fact, he discovered that he had acted like that, when he was in elementary school and his mother returned to work after being a stay-at-home mother since his birth. It was a memory he never thought about, but once he accessed it he recalled feeling abandoned. Too young to understand his feelings, he reacted by ignoring his mother, exaggerating his displeasure, and being mean to her. Years later the memory of that time was activated (unbeknownst to him) and he responded to his wife as if he were a hurt, confused child. After connecting these dots, he was able to learn healthier ways to cope with his wife's transition.

So what does all this mean for you? It means that even though these patterns can seem to run our lives at times, they can be changed. It requires an excavation of sorts—digging around our memories for artifacts of relationships past. From there, we can garner valuable awareness and learn new ways of interacting and reacting.

- What was your role in the relationship?

- Were there issues that kept popping up, again and again?

- What were typical interactions with your significant other like, and were you comfortable with them?

- What part did you play in resolving conflicts?

- What part did you play in creating conflicts?

- What type of partner were you with your significant other(s)?

- Were you able to meet your significant other's relational needs?

- Did your partner feel validated, listened to, and appreciated? If not, why?

- How did you tend to communicate? Were you able to speak openly, honestly, directly and without aggression?

- As you examine yourself during this exercise, did you see any patterns similar to ones in your family of origin, and if so, what were they?

After answering those questions, scan the other important relationships in your life and see if anything stands out as a pattern. You might consider enlisting the help of a therapist in sorting this out, especially if you find yourself in psychologically, emotionally or physically abusive relationships.

Again, the good news is that it's possible to become aware of our relationship patterns and commit to learning to alter them, and, as a result, find freedom from history that gets in the way of healthy relationships in our lives.

Lesson 26: Maturity: Practical Wisdom On Being A Grown-Up

"The mark of the immature man is that he wants to die nobly for a cause, while the mark of the mature man is that he wants to live humbly for one." — J.D. Salinger, The Catcher In The Rye

So many adults live in an emotionally regressed state of mind or existence. What, exactly, does it mean to be a mature adult? Some believe it's a number, an age; some may believe it requires a rite of passage. Here is a list of general traits of those men and women who demonstrate maturity on a mental, emotional, and spiritual level:

- **Take responsibility for your own life.** Do not blame others for your choices, behaviors, actions, or mistakes. Be a man or woman of honor, look yourself in the mirror, and take ownership of who you are.

  "Parents can only give children good advice or put them on the right paths, but the final forming of a person's character lies in their own hands." - Anne Frank

- **Realize growth is a process.** Allow yourself the grace and understanding to learn and grow one day at a time, one circumstance at a time. Becoming a mature adult is a continual process. Big jumps of growth never come; instead, people grow by small increments. If you want to be good at math, do not worry about how big the book is, instead, focus on today's homework.

  "The good life is a process, not a state of being. It is a direction, not a destination." – Carl Rogers

- **Overcome fear.** Fear is common; you will have many opportunities in life to experience it. Overcoming fear does not necessarily mean not feeling fear, rather, it means learning how to succeed in spite of the feeling. The best way to overcome fear is to value courage. If you find yourself feeling afraid, do not give the fear the power; instead, value courage, be brave, and do what is necessary regardless of how you feel. Experience your fears, and go ahead in spite of them.

  "It's OKAY to be scared. Being scared means you're about to do something really, really brave." — Mandy Hale

- **Learn to manage pain.** Self-focused individuals tend to overly emphasize their pains and inconveniences in life, overrating the feelings that cause them to feel uncomfortable. Immature individuals tend to let pain stop them from accomplishing their responsibilities. Rather than avoiding pain, the best approach in maturity is to face it head on, realizing that the pains in life are often the building blocks of wisdom, strength and skill.

"Adversity toughens manhood, and the characteristic of the good or the great man is not that he has been exempt from the evils of life, but that he has surmounted them." – Patrick Henry

- **Be diligent**. Diligence means showing initiative and working hard. Life is not a spectator sport. Maturity requires action. You can dream about life being an adventure, or you can live a life of adventure. Whatever you dream about, take one action-step today to begin the process of reaching your dream. Diligence requires action verbs – study, work, build, invest...

"Diligence is the mother of good luck." – Ben Franklin

- **Know how to properly handle temptation**. Always remember, temptations are invitations to destroy your life. Understand that each temptation you face is designed to destroy some valuable part of you. Every temptation you face is common to mankind. When faced with temptation do three things – (a) flee; (b) ask yourself; "what should I be doing instead right now?" and (c) do something good instead. Do not try to stand up against temptation, telling yourself you should be strong enough to face it; rather, leave the situation immediately.

"I can resist everything except temptation." – Oscar Wilde

- **Manage authority well.** In other words, when you are placed in a position of authority, use this as an instance to lead well, by example. Do not be a person who abuses his authority, by hurting others or by being selfish. When in authority, be a servant leader; that is, instead of saying, "Do this, do that," say instead, "come on, I'll show the way."

"A leader is one who knows the way, goes the way, and shows the way." - John C. Maxwell

- **Be a good life partner**. Not everyone chooses to get married; but if you want to be a person of integrity, with a fulfilling lifelong partner, then prepare yourself for the task. There are three essential ingredients for having a healthy intimate relationship; these are – **listening skills**, **empathy**, and **validation**. Having a fulfilling lifelong relationship requires intimacy – that is being real and vulnerable with one other person; taking off the mask of superficiality and being unwilling to hold the other at arm's length. Healthy connection requires risk. Be the type of person who shows respect, care, and thoughtfulness to the other. Do not go in to the relationship looking for what you can take from the other person; rather look at how you can best love that person.

"Happily ever after is not a fairy tale. It's a choice." – Fawn Weaver

- **Be a lifelong learner**. Education and going to school are not necessarily the same. Even if you have a college degree you may not be learned about the things of life. A good education prepares you for the events that occur in life, and often, the most valuable learning does not occur in the classroom.

  "Education comprehends all that series of instruction and discipline which is intended to enlighten the understanding, correct the temper, and form the manners and habits of youth, and fit them for usefulness in their future stations." – Noah Webster

- **Forgive others**. Do not waste your valuable time ruminating over how others have hurt you. Instead, acknowledge that you have been hurt; process your feelings of anger, betrayal, despair, disappointment, or any other feelings regarding the situation. Make a conscious decision to turn over your negative feelings to God, trusting that you do not have to retaliate or seek restitution from the person who harmed you. Make the choice to have a forgiving heart; open your hands and "let go" of your hurts. This frees up your mind to think and do good.

  "Darkness cannot drive out darkness; only light can do that. Hate cannot drive out hate; only love can do that." - Martin Luther King, Jr.

Lesson 27: Checklist For Recovering Abusers

(Adapted from Lundy Bancroft's *Checklist for Assessing Change in Men who Abuse Women,* 2007)

Use this checklist as a guide to determine your growth and development to becoming a non-abusing person.

- I admit fully to what I have done.

- I no longer make excuses for my behavior

- I do not blame other people for my feelings, attitudes, or behaviors.

- I make amends for the wrongs I have done to anyone I have harmed.

- I accept responsibility for my actions and recognize that abuse is a choice.

- I have identified patterns of my controlling behavior and admit to their wrongness.

- I accept that overcoming abusiveness will be a decades-long process, not just me declaring myself to be cured.

- I have identified the attitudes that drive my abuse.

- I will never say again, "So now it's your turn to do your work," and will not use any of my change as a bargaining chip in my relationship.

- I will not demand any credit for the improvements I have made and I also understand why, if I need to demand any credit; then I have not changed at all. I have merely become more covert in my abusiveness.

- I do not use any of my "improvements" as chips or vouchers to spend on occasional acts of abuse (e.g., "I haven't done anything like this in a long time, so why are you making such a big deal about it?"

- I am developing respectful, kind, supportive behaviors.

- I carry my own weight. I do my fair share of household responsibilities.

- I share power equally with my partner.

- I have changed how I respond in highly heated conflicts. I do not use any abusive tactics, such as bullying, stonewalling, the silent treatment, ignoring, pouting, or anything that is perceived by the other person as hurtful.

- I listen to my partner; I give eye-contact and show interest with my body language.

- I have changed my parenting and I am a non-abusive, involved and engaged parent. I am a good role model to my children.

- I do not have sexist opinions about people of the opposite gender.

- I have changed my attitudes towards others in general.

- I accept the consequences of my actions without feeling sorry for myself. I do not blame my partner or my children (or anyone else) for my consequences.

Lesson 28: Effects On Children

(Story of Emotional Injury and Recovery In Children Exposed To Domestic Abuse, By Lundy Bancroft)

Mariel dreaded each fight that would break out between her parents. She would wish she could magically sail to a warm island, with no sound but the wind blowing in the trees and the birds singing. The mounting tension between Mom and Dad, the voices growing louder, Dad's rage and Mom's panic more palpable with each passing second, all felt so familiar to her that she could almost act out the scenario herself. Yet her heart raced each time, because the ending was unpredictable. Sometimes the yelling would be followed by one parent or the other storming away and slamming a door, and then an hour or two of thick tension would pass, after which life went on as if nothing had happened.

Other times Dad would call Mom crude, demeaning names, or they would both yell mean things at each other, and Dad would scatter a pile of papers into the air with an enraged sweep of his arm and yell; "you're going to be sorry if you don't shut up!" Once, two or three years earlier, and then again only a few weeks ago, Dad had shoved Mom hard, leaving her trembling and choking back her rage.

Mariel was 11 years old, and she had two younger brothers, Joel who was 8 and a half and Marty who was 5. She worried about the boys, because they would get upset when their parents would have loud fights, with Marty sometimes crying and shaking. She was also disturbed by how filled with hatred Joel seemed at times, such as the night a couple of months earlier when he had said to Mariel, "we're big enough now, let's plan a way to kill Dad."

A couple of weeks later, he had said to her, "I mean it Mariel, if he makes Mom cry one more time, I am going to beat his brains in with my baseball bat while he's sleeping." Marty had overheard what Joel said, and started to have violent nightmares.

One night Mariel woke up to hear her parents fighting in their bedroom. "I'm sick of this, Kaleigh," her father was yelling, "it's been weeks! I don't want to hear any more of your fucking excuses about how your head aches or you're too tired. I know you've got something going with that guy you work with — I'm not an idiot, you know! That's why you don't want it with me anymore! You're all kissy and lovey-dovey with the children, but you don't give a shit about me, do you? Well I'm out of here, you fucking bitch. By the time I get back here tomorrow, I'd better not find you here, or you'll be sorry. You can go sleep under a bridge for all I care."

Mariel could then hear drawers opening and slamming, and the sound of glass smashing, followed by her father's car screeching out of the driveway. She quickly went to comfort her brothers, and she found Marty pale and trembling. Her mother did not come out of her room. Mariel stayed with Joel and Marty and eventually fell asleep in Marty's bed with him, drifting off into a night of haunted dreams that left her drained and pale.

The children were woken by their mother at the usual time, and the preparations for school followed the normal routine, but Mom was off in another world. Her lip seemed to quiver slightly when she spoke. As she was saying good-bye to the children, she told them, "Don't get on the bus after school. I'm going to pick you up."

That afternoon, Mom arrived at the school with a car full of packed suitcases. The children were startled. "We're going to stay at Aunt Sheila's for a few days," she explained. "We need to take a little trip, because she needs me to help her with some things." But it was obvious to the children that they were fleeing because of the previous night's fight. They sat in stunned silence during much of the two-hour drive.

During the days that they stayed at their aunt's house, the children heard Mom crying several times. One day she left them in Sheila's care for several hours, saying that she had some errands to run. (But in fact she was going to court to obtain an order removing their father from the home because of his threats.)

A few days later — once Kaleigh received confirmation from the police that Felix had been served the protective order — they drove back home and resumed their daily routine. Only Dad wasn't there anymore. Mom explained to them, "We need some time apart to work things out so that we won't fight so much." They wanted to know how long Dad would be away, but she had to tell them that she didn't really know. "A few weeks maybe, or a couple of months" she said evasively. Marty cried for his father at bedtime every evening for the next several days.

Mariel and Joel both felt a flood of relief, bordering on elation. "I can't believe that fucker is finally out of here!" Joel said to his sister, "I hope we never see him again. I hate him." Mariel responded with sharp disapproval; "don't talk about Dad like that. You don't hate him, you love him." Joel shot back at her, "Love him? You're crazy! All he ever does is yell at people and put them down. It's much better without him. Don't be stupid."

For a few days, the house was peaceful. They spoke to each other in soft voices, they snuggled close on the couch to read stories, and they watched movies without interruptions. They felt happy.

But happiness began to have its price. Mariel worried about how her father was doing, and she felt guilty for being so happy about his absence. Joel started to feel that his resentments towards Dad had driven him away (though this belief might seem illogical to an adult). And Marty sometimes wanted everything back the way it was, simply because that was the life he was familiar with.

For several weeks, Felix made no effort to see the children, or even to contact them by telephone. He felt too bitter and upset, and would tell friends and relatives, "they all ganged up against me together. She has brainwashed the children to think everything is my fault."

Joel made a point of saying to Mariel, and to his mother, "who cares if he calls? He should go to hell." But in reality he felt abandoned by his father, and worried that maybe Dad hated him for taking his mother's side. Marty cried less often for Dad than at first, but began instead to talk incessantly about him, turning him into an almost mythical figure: "daddy is a pilot now, he flies all over the world"; "Daddy is going to come for us one day and take us to meet the President"; "daddy had to do some really important secret work, and they're going to pay him tons of money."

With Felix out of the house, Mariel's relationship with her mother became better in some ways and more difficult in others. Mom was noticeably more patient and less grouchy. She would even smile and laugh sometimes, and the attention she paid the children was more focused than they could remember in many years. But Mariel was put off by her sense that Mom was starting to act less like a troubled friend who needed Mariel's support and assistance, and more like — well, more like a *mother*. She was imposing more discipline, and she was keeping her private thoughts more to herself, confiding in other people instead of Mariel.

Mariel wasn't sure she liked this change. She didn't want her mother to have a kind of authority that Mariel wasn't used to, and she felt somewhat pushed away emotionally. Yet at the same time her mother seemed more present and loving. The changes left Mariel feeling confused.

After two or three months had gone by, the relaxed and cooperative atmosphere in the home began to deteriorate. The children's complicated and often contradictory emotions about their parents' separation began to erupt in various ways. Back when their father was still living at home, the children had for years stuffed away their bitterness, sadness, and fear about the abuse of Mom that they heard and saw, and the times when dad targeted them directly for his unkindness. This backlog of distress was now tightly interwoven with their upset and guilt about the recent changes.

And now that Dad wasn't in the home anymore, and with Mom visibly stronger and happier, the children felt safe to let loose demons they had been keeping tightly caged. Mariel, who for years had been hyper-mature, like a second mother in the house, started regressing into whining and demanding. She wanted help choosing her clothes in the morning, complained that she didn't understand any of her homework, and became unable to fall asleep without her mother.

Marty couldn't settle down at night, convinced that a monster was going to come to the house to kill them all. The slightest disappointment or frustration would send him into sobs or tantrums.

The direction that Joel was taking was perhaps the most worrisome. Since roughly three years earlier, he had shown a tendency to pick up certain aspects of his father's conduct, particularly the swearing and yelling. But he had rarely exhibited that behavior when Dad was around, since he was afraid of being punished. With Dad now out of the picture, though, Joel felt emboldened, and he not only became more frequently mouthy and defiant, he also developed an array of new ways of being disrespectful to his mother, most of which looked hauntingly similar to Felix's style. He would, for example, mimic his mother's voice to insult her when she was angry, call her "stupid idiot," and scold her like a small child when he didn't feel catered to — such as times when she sent him to school with lunches that weren't his favorite.

In a peak of frustration one day, Kaleigh yelled at her son, "You're turning out just like your father!" Joel shot back, "fuck you!". Kaleigh was so shocked by her son's vulgarity that she slapped him across the face. Joel was deeply hurt by his mother's words, and by being hit, but he was determined not to let his emotional wound show, and instead became even more superior and demeaning.

Kaleigh felt overwhelmed by her children's unexpected emotional and behavioral backsliding. Her own recovery could have been a full-time job, but she had to support her children economically and care for them on top of everything that was stirring inside of her. Her inner turmoil was following a trajectory similar to her children's; her initial elation and sense of freedom from getting away from Felix was giving way to rage, sleeplessness, and anxiety about the future. *Both Mom and children were, in short, experiencing how distance from trauma can create a space to begin feeling its true impact, a natural stage in the healing process.*

No one had provided Kaleigh a map to the terrain she was crossing, and she made numerous errors as she worked her way through, such as the time she slapped Joel. She could be grouchy and short-tempered with the children, and sometimes blamed them for not being more appreciative of how hard she had been fighting to get the three of them into better circumstances. There were days when she felt that she couldn't listen to the three of them cry at bedtime anymore, or squabble with each other all afternoon, and would yell at them to snap out of it. At times she drifted off into her fear and bitterness about her years with Felix, and about having to be the healer of the psychological harm to the children that he had left in his wake.

But she didn't give up. She would apologize to her children when she needed to, and work hard to do better the next day. She told Joel she was wrong to slap him, and that he was *not* just like his father. At the same time, she kept setting limits with her children, requiring them to behave respectfully toward her and guiding them to overcome the negative attitudes they had absorbed from Felix. She began rebuilding a social life for herself so that she had people to talk with about the hard but satisfying life of a single mother building a life of freedom. And her tenacity bore fruit; by the time they had been out from under Felix's heavy hand for five or six months, they were starting to get back toward calm and closeness. Healing was unfolding as it should.

About nine months after the separation, Felix suddenly reappeared, demanding to have the children on weekends and a couple of evenings during the week. Kaleigh resisted, since the children were now doing so well, and Felix took the matter to court. Kaleigh explained to the judge that the children were recovering well from their exposure to his abusive behavior but still needed more time of peace and quiet, and that Felix had vanished for almost a year, so she didn't see why it was so urgent to him now to have so much time with the children. She also asked that his visits with the children be supervised.

Felix responded that Kaleigh's allegations of abuse were completely trumped up as a way to keep him away from the children because she was upset that Felix had a new girlfriend. He said that she had actually been the one with the abuse problem, and claimed that Kaleigh had hit him several times and used to hit the children. He said that the reason he had stayed away for nine months was because she had completely turned the children against him and he had "given up hope," but that now he wanted to try again to prove to his children that he was not the monster she was telling them he was.

He told the judge he would be happy to pay child support; "I of course want to contribute to my children financially, I'm their father." The judge was impressed at Felix's commitment to be an involved father, and made no issue of the fact that Felix hadn't sent any support during his absence.

Felix was granted unsupervised visitation On Tuesday and Thursday afternoons, with overnights on alternate weekends. The judge said, "I don't know whether to believe these abuse charges, but anyhow that has nothing to do with the children. The children need to have close relationships with both of you. I'm not going to deny Felix the opportunity to be back in their lives."

The children were happy that Felix had returned to them. For the first few months he put a great deal of energy into making the visits fun, and was much more patient with the children that he had been when the family was together. Joel went from despising his father to declaring that his father was a great person; "He's really changed, Mom, he's completely different from how he was before." Felix explained this transformation to his children by telling them that he had just needed to get away from the stress of the terrible relationship he and Kaleigh had shared.

Felix's new partner, June, was kind to the children, and was very impressed by what a great father Felix was. June was disgusted that Kaleigh would try to restrict the children's contact with him, and that she would call during visits to check up on how they were doing.

All three of the children regressed emotionally and behaviorally as contact with their father resumed. Joel returned to imitating his father's disparaging and bullying behavior toward his mother, and Mariel drifted back into bottling up her feelings and looking after her younger brothers. Marty resumed having trouble falling asleep at night and biting his nails during the day. Kaleigh complained to the court of these effects, but the court social worker told her that the children were just struggling with the transitions in their lives, and that they felt caught in the middle between the two warring parents. She said that they were probably reacting largely to Kaleigh's hostility toward Felix rather than to feelings of their own, since they obviously loved their father and were eager to see him.

As the months went by, the children began to come home with distressing reports about certain aspects of their visits. They would report that Felix had made an insulting comment to his new partner June, or Mariel would express upset that her father had punished Marty too harshly and that he would call Joel a "spaz" when they played whiffle ball. One night Marty cried at bedtime, telling his mother that when they were on visits, Felix and June would make "mean jokes" about Kaleigh, and that Mariel and Joel would laugh about the jokes, "but they make me feel sad."

When Kaleigh would ask the children to explain more about any of these events, they would clam up. They felt loyal to their father, and they also worried that if they revealed the worst aspects of his behavior they would lose him again. They were swayed further by his steady stream of spending on them, buying them boom boxes, dirt bikes, and other expensive enticements, and taking them on costly outings to restaurants and amusement parks.

After several months of growing closer to her father, Mariel began to pull away again, and after a year or so told her mother that she wished she didn't have to go on visits with him at all, "because he says mean things to the boys or to June, and sometimes he makes fun of me, like about me being so skinny." Yet Mariel would never skip a visit, and Kaleigh became increasingly convinced that she was afraid to leave her younger brothers alone with their father.

Kaleigh did not want to speak badly about the children's father to them, but she also could tell that they needed help in making sense out of their conflicted feelings, the strong affection they held for him that collided with his periodic selfish or mean actions. Watching Mariel become once again burdened, seeing Joel taking up the role of mini-abuser that he had overcome, wincing as Marty descended back into insecurity, Kaleigh felt anguished. Would her beloved children be able to get through this next phase, which seemed as hard as any they had faced? Was she going to lose her closeness with them, as they drifted off into secret-keeping about their visits?

Kaleigh found herself in a quandary about how to guide her children through these treacherous waters. It was clear that, at least for now, the court was not going to permit her to restrict her children's exposure to Felix's abusiveness and manipulation, and to the reawakening of traumatic memories which his current behavior caused them. Kaleigh wished urgently to protect her children, and began searching in every direction she could think of for an avenue that was open to her.

Lesson 29: The Batterer As Parent

(Adapted from Lundy Bancroft (2002)

Research on children's exposure to domestic violence has tended to focus primarily on two aspects of their experience: the trauma of witnessing physical assaults against their mother, and the tension produced by living with a high level of conflict between their parents.1 However, these are just two elements of a much deeper problem pervading these children's daily life, which is that they are living with a batterer. The parenting of men who batterer exposes children to multiple potential sources of emotional and physical injury, most of which have not been recognized widely.

This section looks at the characteristics of men who batter and identifies ways in which these characteristics also influence their ability to parent appropriately. Additionally, the section will address the implications of such parenting for child protective and custody determinations.

Characteristics of Men Who Batter

Most of the characteristics that are typical of men who batter have potential ramifications for children in the home. Batterers often tend toward authoritarian, neglectful, and verbally abusive child-rearing. The effects on the children of these and other parenting weaknesses may be intensified by the children's prior traumatic experience of witnessing violence. Consider the following selected examples of characteristics of men who batter:

Control: Coerciveness is widely recognized as a central quality of battering men, and one of the areas of life heavily controlled by many men who batterer is the mother's parenting. A man who batters may cause or forbid his partner to terminate a pregnancy, overrule her parenting decisions, or assault her when he is angry over the children's behavior. Battered women are far more likely than other mothers to feel that they have to alter their parenting styles when their partners are present.

Entitlement: A man who batters considers himself entitled to a special status within the family, with the right to use violence when he deems it necessary. This outlook of entitlement can lead to selfish and self-centered behavior on his part. For example, he may become irate or violent when he feels that his partner is paying more attention to the children than to him. It is difficult for children to have their needs met in such an atmosphere and they are vulnerable to role-reversal, where they are made to feel responsible to take care of the battering parent.

Possessiveness: Men who batter often have been observed to perceive their partners as owned objects. This possessive outlook can sometimes extend to their children, partly accounting for the dramatically elevated rates of physical abuse and sexual abuse of children perpetrated by batterers, and for the fact that these men seek custody of their children more often than non-battering fathers do.

Other characteristics that can have an important impact on children include **manipulativeness**, **denial** and **minimization** of the abuse, **battering in multiple relationships**, and **resistance to change**.

Influence of Battering On Parenting

The characteristics discussed above influence the parenting of men who batter and have a negative impact on the children by:

- Creating role models that perpetuate the violence

- Undermining the mother's authority

- Retaliating against the mother for her efforts to protect the children

- Sowing divisions within the family

- Using the children as weapons against the mother

Creating role models that perpetuate the violence: Boys who are exposed to domestic violence show dramatically elevated rates of battering their own partners as adolescents or adults. Research suggests that this connection is a product more of the values and attitudes that boys learn from witnessing battering behavior than of the emotional trauma of being exposed to such abuse. Daughters of battered women show increased difficulty in escaping partner abuse in their adult relationships. Both boys and girls have been observed to accept various aspects of the batterer's belief-system, including the view that victims of violence are to blame, that women exaggerate hysterically when they report abuse, and that males are superior to females.

Undermining the mother's authority: Domestic violence is inherently destructive to maternal authority because the batterer's verbal abuse and violence provide a model for children of contemptuous and aggressive behavior toward their mother. The predictable result, confirmed by many studies, is that children of battered women have increased rates of violence and disobedience toward their mothers. Some battered mothers make reports of being prevented from picking up a crying infant or from assisting a frightened or injured child and of being barred from providing other basic physical, emotional, or even medical care. Interference of this kind can cause the children to feel that their mother does not care about them or is unreliable. The batterer may reinforce those feelings by verbally conditioning the children through statements such as; "your mother doesn't love you," or, "Mommy only cares about herself."

Retaliating against her for her efforts to protect the children: A mother may find that she is assaulted or intimidated if she attempts to prevent the batterer from mistreating the children, or may find that he harms the children more seriously to punish her for standing up for them. Therefore, she may be forced over time to stop intervening on her children's behalf. This dynamic can lead children to perceive their mother as uncaring about the batterer's mistreatment of them, and can contribute to her being labeled by child protective services as "failing to protect."

Sowing divisions with the family: Some batterers use favoritism to build a special relationship with one child in the family. As some researchers have noted, the favored child is particularly likely to be a boy, and the batterer may bond with him partly through encouraging a sense of superiority to females. Batterers also may create or feed familial tensions deliberately. These manipulative behaviors are a likely factor in the high rate of inter-sibling conflict and violence observed in families exposed to battering behavior.

Using the children as weapons: Many men who batter use children as a vehicle to harm or control the mother through such tactics as destroying the children's belongings to punish the mother, requiring the children to monitor and report on their mother's activities, or threatening to kidnap or take custody of the children if the mother attempts to end the relationship. These parenting behaviors draw the children into the abuser's behavior pattern. Post-separation, many batterers use unsupervised visitation as an opportunity to further abuse the mother through the children.

Lesson 30: Emotional Engagement Inventory For Perpetrators Of Violence

(Source: Dr. Sue Johnson, *Hold Me Tight,* 2008*)*

A.R.E. is an acronym describing the questions deeply embedded in the hearts of every person in a love relationship. As you read the following descriptions, ask yourself how you can be the type of partner your loved one needs.

A: Accessibility – Can I reach you?

Are you able to be emotionally present for your partner even when you are feeling emotionally overwhelmed yourself? How can you step back from disconnection and tune in to your lover's attachment cues?

R: Responsiveness – Can I rely on you to respond to me emotionally?

This means tuning in to your partner's needs and fears and showing your partner that his or her emotions have an impact on you. It means accepting and placing a priority on the emotional signals your partner is conveying and responding with clear signals of comfort and care when your partner needs them.

Sensitive responsiveness always calms us both emotionally and on a physical level.

E: Engagement – Do I know you will value me and stay close?

Engagement is the same as emotional presence. Are you able to attune to your partner's emotional cues and remain sensitively available to him or her?

Take the ARE Questionnaire:

From your viewpoint are you *accessible* to your partner?

1. My partner can get positive attention easily from me.   T   F

2. I am easy to connect with emotionally.   T   F

3. I show my partner that he/she comes first with me.   T   F

4. I do not shut my partner out and cause him/her to feel lonely in this relationship.   T   F

5. My partner can share his/her deepest feelings with me I will listen. I will not use what he/she shares with me as a weapon later.   T   F

From your viewpoint are you *responsive* to your partner?

1. If my partner needs connection and comfort, I will be there for him/her.   T   F

2. I respond to signals that my partner needs me to come close.   T   F

3. My partner can lean on me when he/she is anxious or unsure.   T   F

4. Even when we fight or disagree, my partner knows that he/she is important to me and we will find a way to come together.   T F

5. If my partner needs reassurance about how important he/she is to me, I can give it.   T F

Are you positively emotionally *engaged* with each other?

1. I feel very comfortable being close to, trusting my partner.   T F

2. My partner feels comfortable being close to and trusting me.   T F

3. I can confide in my partner about almost anything.   T F

4. My partner can confide in me about almost anything.   T F

5. I feel confident, even when we are apart, that we are connected to each other.   T F

6. I know that my partner cares about my joys, hurts, and fears.   T F

7. I care about my partner's joys, hurts, and fears.   T F

8. I feel safe enough to take emotional risks with my partner.   T F

9. My partner feels safe enough to take emotional risks with me.   T F

A score of 10 or above indicates a secure bond.

Take an emotional connectedness inventory:

In love relationships it is important to learn how to create positive dependency and how to care for each other with emotional responsiveness on a daily basis. Take the following inventory to help understand yourself with respect to this concept of emotional intimacy and healthy attachment.

- What messages about love/marriage did you get from your parents orour community? Was being able to reach for and trust others seen as a strength and a resource?

- Before your present relationship, did you experience a safe, loving relationship with someone you trusted, felt close to, and could turn to if needed? Do you have an image of what this looks like in your head, a model that can help you as you create your present relationship?

- Did your past relationships teach you that loved ones were unreliable and that you had to be vigilant and fight to be seen and responded to? Or did you learn that depending on others is dangerous and it is best to distance yourself, to not need others, and to avoid closeness?

- What strategies did you learn to use in past relationships, say, with your parents, when things started to go wrong?

- Can you remember a time when you really needed to know a loved one was with you? If he or she was not, what was that like for you and what did you learn from it? How did you cope? Does this have an impact on your relationships now?

- If it is hard for you to turn to and trust others, to let them close when you really need them, what do you do when life gets too big to handle or when you feel alone?

- Name two very concrete and specific things that a safe, accessible, responsive, and engaged lover in a relationship with you would do on a typical day and how those things would make you feel at that moment?

- In your present relationship, can you ask your partner, let him/her see, when you need closeness and comfort? Is this easy for you or difficult to do? Perhaps this feels like a sign of weakness for you, or maybe it just feels too risky. Rate your difficulty in doing this on a scale from 1 to 10. A high score means this is very difficult for you to do.

- When you feel disconnected or alone in your present relationships, are you likely to get very emotional or anxious? Do you push your partner to respond? Or are you more likely to shut down and try not to feel your need to connect? Can you think of a time when this happened?

- Think of a time in your relationship when questions like, "Are you there for me?" were hanging in the air unanswered and you wound up getting into a fight about a mundane problem. Talk about this experience.

- Can you think of bonding moments in your relationship when one of you reaches out and the other responds in a way that makes you both feel emotionally connected and secure with each other?

Lesson 31: Domestic Violence and Substance Abuse

While substance abuse does not cause domestic violence, say the experts, there is a statistical correlation between the two issues. What studies of domestic violence have found is that there is frequent high incidence of alcohol and other drug use by perpetrators during domestic abuse. The reality is that not only do batterers tend to abuse drugs and alcohol, but the probability that victims of domestic violence will turn to alcohol and drugs to cope with the abuse increases as well.

Delving into what's known about the two issues — domestic violence and substance abuse — can shed some light on the problem that affects so many in the U.S.

- Regular alcohol abuse is one of the leading risk factors for partner violence (between spouses or partners).

- When there is a battering incident coupled with alcohol abuse, the battering may be more severe and result in greater injury to the victim or victims.

- Studies of alcoholic women indicate that they are more likely to report they've had childhood physical and emotional abuse than women who are nonalcoholic.

- In fact, women who have been abused are 15 times more likely to abuse alcohol and nine times more likely to abuse drugs than women who have not been abused.

- Relative to the type of childhood abuse suffered, the National Center on Addiction and Substance Abuse found that 69% of women being treated for substance abuse reported they were sexually abused as children.

- Treatment for alcoholism does not cure abusive behavior.

- The Department of Justice found in 2002 that 36% of victims in domestic violence programs also had problems with substance abuse.

- According to a majority of domestic violence program directors (51%), a woman's use of alcohol can be a barrier to her being able to leave a violent relationship with a spouse or partner.

- An even greater percentage (87%) of domestic violence program directors agree with the statement that the risk of intimate partner violence increases when both partners abuse drugs or alcohol.

Perhaps the most heartbreaking consequence of the dual issues of domestic violence and substance abuse is what happens to the children involved. Instead of being nurtured, children living in abusive homes where drugs and alcohol abuse occur simultaneously are often deprived of more than just the basics of food and shelter. They may face lifelong consequences resulting from parents who abuse substances and resort to violence.

It's a fact that children of substance abusing parents are more likely to experience physical, emotional, or sexual abuse than children who live in non-substance abusing homes. In a survey conducted by the National Committee to Prevent Child Abuse, the results showed that as many as 80% of child abuse cases were linked with drug and alcohol use.

It is estimated that three million children witness violent acts against their mothers each year. As a result, many of them may come to believe that behaving in a violent manner is an acceptable way of expressing control, anger or frustration.

And violence carried across generations – victims of abuse themselves abusing partners and offspring in the future – is estimated to be 30-40% in the general population. This suggests that up to four in every 10 children who either witness or experience violence in the family unit run an increased risk of becoming involved in a violent relationship when they are adults.

The batterers often exhibit profound remorse over what they've done, promising to never do it again, blaming the alcohol or drugs. But the truth is that domestic violence never just goes away. And it won't stop just because the person doing the battering stops using alcohol or drugs.

Even when the substance abusing batterer goes into treatment for substance abuse, treatment for that alone will not curtail the abuse. Both need to be treated simultaneously. Unfortunately, too many people believe that it's just the drugs or alcohol that causes the violence. The tragic result is that the batterer, once rehab is complete, still has the underlying psychological impulse to abuse his (or her) spouse and/or children. Without treatment to overcome those urges, the violence will simply continue. The bottom line is that one problem (substance abuse or domestic violence) cannot be addressed without also dealing with the other.

Many victims of domestic violence who abuse substances suffer from post-traumatic stress syndrome (PTSD). Treatment for PTSD may occur in-house during residential treatment, or the woman can be referred to the appropriate provider for PTSD treatment. One effective treatment for PTSD is eye movement desensitization and reprocessing (EMDR).

Victims of childhood or other trauma may benefit from specific trauma treatment by a therapist specializing in treating victims of childhood abuse.

Similar to individuals seeking treatment for substance abuse, when a person enters treatment for substance abuse who is a batterer, he or she is likely in a crisis state. He may have been referred to the treatment program by the courts after being arrested for drug- or violence-related charges. He may have been left alone by his partner and children after they sought safety from his physical and emotional violence. In any case, the danger of violence erupting is always present.

Fostering accountability is of vital importance in successful treatment. Experts say that the degree to which a batterer begins to assume responsibility for his actions can serve as a barometer for his progress during substance abuse treatment.

Referral to and collaboration with batterer's intervention programs can help facilitate treatment for substance abuse in batterers. The relationship between substance abuse and violent behavior needs to be examined. Answers to the following questions can help treatment providers prepare an appropriate treatment plan:

- Exactly when, in relation to an instance of substance abuse, does the violence occur?

- How much of the violent behavior occurs when the individual is drinking or using drugs?

- What substances are used before the violent act?

- What feelings precede or accompany the use of drugs or alcohol?

- Is alcohol or drugs used to recover from an incident of violence?

Other areas of treatment typically include bonding with peers and parenting classes. There is also a focus on the matter of ongoing support for the substance-abusing batterers. While there are many national 12 step groups for those in recovery from alcohol, drugs, gambling, compulsive sexual behavior and other disorders, there are no ongoing organizations that support change for men who batter, nor their surviving victims.

Shining a spotlight on domestic violence, the hidden side of substance abuse, isn't easy. The victims are understandably reticent about coming forward. Fearing for their safety, they may be unwilling or unable to get treatment or help for themselves. Batterers who also abuse substances are unlikely to be forthcoming about their violent behavior. But with the prevalence of domestic violence and substance abuse in today's society necessitates continued intervention, prevention, treatment and recovery services.

Lesson 32: Harmful Behavior

(Source: Emerge Domestic Violence Prevention Education)

What counts as harmful behavior?

In general, harmful behavior constitutes any action which causes pain or harm in someone else. As you can imagine, there is an infinite number of actions which have the potential to cause pain or harm, and many of those actions are not necessarily intentional. At Emerge, we look at both intentional and unintentional actions which may become a harmful pattern of behavior.

The following list contains some examples of harmful, abusive, controlling, and violent behavior, as well as the effects that this behavior may have caused. If you have done anything on this list to a partner, chances are that you understand the damage that these actions can cause. At Emerge we ask group members to identify how they have harmed others so that they can work to keep it from happening again.

Have you ever hit, pushed, grabbed, threatened, frightened or intimidated your partner?

Is your partner afraid of you?

Are your children afraid of you?

Are you concerned that your behavior is harming your relationship?

Have you broken promises about changing behavior?

Have you ever punched a wall, banged a table, or broken something during a disagreement?

Have you ever grabbed your partner during a disagreement, attempted to stop her/him from leaving, locked her/him out, or restrained her/him in any way?

Do you pressure your partner to do things your way, even when you know your partner doesn't want to?

Has your partner ever said 'you're always trying to control me'?

Do you use names, put-downs or swearing to control your partner?

Do you put the blame onto your partner for things you are responsible for?

Have you found yourself 'keeping score' of the wrongs your partner has done to you in order to hold those things against her/him?

Have you ever blamed your abusive actions on alcohol, other drugs, stress or family problems?

Have you cheated on your partner or been sexually abusive in other ways?

Have you ever been accused of mistreating your children?

Are you concerned that your children are being emotionally or psychologically harmed because of the way you treat your partner?

Has your partner complained about jealous or possessive behavior on your part?

When you do something that hurts your partner, do you just say "I'm sorry" and then expect acceptance of your apology without making any change in how you were hurtful?

Do you make your partner do things even though you know your partner doesn't want to?

Has your partner ever said 'you're always trying to control me'?

Do you use names, put-downs or swearing to control your partner?

Do you put the blame onto your partner for things you are responsible for?

Have you found yourself 'keeping score' of the wrongs your partner has done to you in order to hold those things against her/him?

Have you ever blamed your abusive actions on alcohol, other drugs, stress or family problems?

Have you cheated on your partner or been sexually abusive in other ways?

Have you ever been accused of mistreating your children?

Are you concerned that your children are being emotionally or psychologically harmed because of the way you treat your partner?

Has your partner complained about jealous or possessive behavior on your part?

When you do something that hurts your partner, do you just say "I'm sorry" and then expect acceptance of your apology without making any change in how you were hurtful?

Lesson 33: The Duluth Model Control Log

(Source: Pope & Ferraro, 2006)

A Straight forward listing of battering behaviors does not help us understand the intent and effect of the choice to use those behaviors. It is through the use of a Control Log that it becomes apparent that it is the totality of behaviors that is abusive and there is an intention to using these behaviors.

Battering behaviors happen because of a belief system that men learn in their culture.

"The abuser bases his actions on two beliefs:

1. First, that he has the right to control his partner's activities, feelings, or thoughts, and
2. Second, that violence is a legitimate method of achieving that control."

There are a number of beliefs held by batterers. Batterers often believe women are manipulators who lie, cheat, steal, exploit them economically, or say no when they mean yes.

Batterers can blame women for violence by believing them to be provocateurs, equally violent, or looking to be dominated.

Batterers believe that there is no alternative to violence; violence is an appropriate response when they feel hurt; or is caused by external factors such as alcohol use or a breakdown in communication.

In relationships, batterers believe that one person needs to be in control, jealousy is an expression of love; and as a male he is entitled to certain rights. This belief system allows the batterer to divert responsibility and provides justification for the continued use of battering behaviors.

A batterer's belief that male privilege is natural validates his sense of entitlement to certain rights in his relationships with women. In the family hierarchy "these include the right to be in charge, to control what his partner does, thinks and feels, and to be the center of things."

"He feels entitled to establish and maintain his position through any means, including the use of violence."

According to the Duluth Model, the use of violence is not due to mental illness, substance abuse, or uncontrolled anger. "This program in all its aspects rejects the notion of men as victims of sexism."

Violence against women is a choice that is socially and institutionally sanctioned, compatible with gender and familial roles, and legitimized by belief systems.

The consciousness of both men and women in this society is shaped by their experiences of this system and all of the forces that work within it. Yet not all men batter women even though all men have been socialized in a society that grants them certain gender privileges.

It is clear that if the batterer is viewed only as a victim of cultural influences and socialization, then there is no place for individual responsibility. **It is only accepting responsibility that makes behavioral change possible.**

Analysis of Duluth Model written materials offers four additional insights:

1. Not all batterers or all violence is the same. The effectiveness of specific tactics may vary from relationship to relationship, yet each batterer determines the level and severity needed to gain and maintain control.
   Men who batter their partners shift tactics according to what they believe will work in a given situation, the mood they're in, the response they're looking for from their partner, or the environment in which they are attempting to exercise control.

   For example, an abuser may use violence in private, but in public may use a certain glare, a threatening gesture, or a humiliating remark. The abuser employs tactics not only to gain his partner's submission to a specific demand, but also to establish a relationship that he can rely upon in the future.
   These tactics appear to be random and unexplainable, but in the context of attempting to establish power in a relationship, random acts of violence are fully explainable.

2. Patterns in individual relationships can also be adapted to meet changing conditions. In interviews with women using the court system, forty-eight percent reported increases in other controlling tactics as the physical violence decreased.

   Each woman's experience can only be understood by exploring the distinct patterns occurring in the specific context of her relationship.

3. Battering takes many forms and is customized in each relationship.

4. Rather than focusing on "why she stays," or focusing on the relationship, it is beneficial to focus on, "how does he batter." In other words, focus on the batterer's beliefs, attitudes, and behaviors.

The Control Log can help batterers analyze their behaviors and hopefully begin to make healthy, non-violent choices in their intimate relationships.

The Control Log

Date_____

1. ACTIONS: Briefly describe the situation and the action you used to control (statements,gestures, tone of voice, physical contact, facial expressions)

_____

_____

2. INTENT: What did you want to happen in this situation?

_____

_____

3. FEELINGS: What feelings were you having?

_____

_____

4. MINIMIZATION, DENIAL AND BLAME: In what ways did you minimize or deny your

actions or blame her?

_____

_____

5. EFFECTS: What was the impact of your action? Include results of blaming or minimizing (On You)(On Her)(On others)

_____

_____

6. PAST VIOLENCE: How did your past use of violence affect this situation?

_____

_____

7. NON-CONTROLLING BEHAVIORS: What could you have done differently?

_____

_____

Lesson 34: Emotional Abuse

Emotional abuse includes non-physical behaviors such as threats, insults, constant monitoring or "checking in," excessive texting, humiliation, intimidation, isolation or stalking.

There are many behaviors that qualify as emotional or verbal abuse:

Please note: this list is not exhaustive, but merely a sample of some of the behaviors that are emotionally abusive. The following list shows some common forms of emotional and verbally abusive behavior. As you read this list, take note of whether you have committed any of these behaviors and attitudes toward your partner (or anyone else.)

- Calling someone names and putting him/her down.

- Yelling and screaming at the other person.

- Intentionally embarrassing him/her in public.

- Preventing him/her from seeing or talking with friends and family.

- Telling the other person what to do and wear.

- Using online communities or cell phones to control, intimidate or humiliate someone.

- Blaming the other person's actions for your abusive or unhealthy behavior.

- Stalking hem/her.

- Threatening to commit suicide to keep the other person from breaking up with you.

- Threatening to harm your partner, their pet, or people your partner cares about.

- Making him/her feel guilty or immature when they don't consent to sexual activity.

- Threatening to expose their secrets such as their sexual orientation or immigration status.

- Starting rumors about them.

- Threatening to have their children taken away.

Is emotional abuse really abuse?

A relationship can be unhealthy or abusive even without physical violence.

Verbal abuse may not cause physical damage,but it does cause emotional pain and scarring. It can also lead to physical violence if the relationship continues on the unhealthy path it's on.

The aim of emotional or psychological abuse is to chip away at the other person's feelings of self-worth and independence. If you're the victim of emotional abuse, you may feel that there is no way out of the relationship, or that without your abusive partner you have nothing.

If you are the abusive person in this relationship, you may feel that you have a right to say mean things and "vent" as long as you aren't using physical violence. This is incorrect.

Emotional abuse includes verbal abuse such as yelling, name-calling, blaming, and shaming. Isolation, intimidation, and controlling behavior also fall under emotional abuse.

Additionally, abusers who use emotional or psychological abuse often throw in threats of physical violence. You may think that physical abuse is far worse than emotional abuse, since physical violence can send a person to the hospital and leave them with scars. But, the scars of emotional abuse are very real, and they run deep.

In fact, emotional abuse can be just as damaging as physical abuse—sometimes even more so. Furthermore, emotional abuse usually worsens over time, often escalating to physical battery.

Sometimes verbal abuse is so bad that the victim actually start believing what the abuser says. The victim begins to think he/she's stupid, ugly or fat. He/she believes that he/she is unlovable. Constantly being criticized and told they aren't good enough causes them to lose confidence and lowers their self-esteem. As a result, victims often start to blame themselves for their partner's abusive behavior.

Remember -- emotional abuse is never the victim's fault. In fact, victims are often just being controlled and manipulated into staying in the relationship.

Lesson 35: Your Behavior Is A Choice

(Source: L. Bancroft, *Guide for Men Who Are Serious About Changing – Part 2*

Making excuses for poor behavior:
Men who harm their partners, whether emotionally, physically, or sexually, tend to see themselves as out of control, and as just reacting to circumstances that are beyond their control. Consider whether you have made any of the following excuses:

"I was so drunk I didn't know what I was doing."

"I was in a rage, and I just lashed out."

"There's only so much a man can take."

"What you were doing reminded me of what my mom used to do to me, and I went berserk."

"You can't expect me to be perfect when I'm that upset."

"The stress of losing my job made me go on a binge."

"I didn't realize what I was doing. I was out of my mind."

"I was in a blackout."

"You know how to totally push my buttons, then you blame me when I go off."

"I would never have slept with that girl if you weren't being so cold to me."

These excuses are all ways of covering up problems and placing the blame or bad behavior on someone or something else. The reality is that the behavior of human beings is not "on automatic"; people *make choices* even when they are deeply hurt, enraged, triggered, or drunk. Even in the highest-pressure situations, people's behavior is shaped by:

- Their attitudes and values about what is acceptable behavior

- Their spiritual and religious beliefs

- Their desire to avoid harming *themselves*

- Their desire to protect belongings that they care about

- Their wish to protect their reputation (how they are viewed by friends, relatives, and the wider public) and to avoid criticism

- Their awareness of possible legal consequences for certain acts

- Their *goals*—what they are trying to accomplish with their behavior

Here are some real-life examples from cases we've been involved with:

Kyle, who said that the pain of his terrible relationship with his wife drove him into cheating on her, and that it was the waves of intense emotion he was having about her that caused him to use such terrible judgment. Yet he also admitted that getting together secretly with his mistress required lots of advance planning, careful lying, faking sickness, and other stratagems that showed he was anything but "out of control."

Brian, who said, "I don't know what I'm doing after six or eight drinks," yet always managed to continue selling weed no matter how drunk he was, without losing any of his skill as a businessperson, without losing his money or his merchandise, and without getting himself arrested.

Marshall, who came home extremely drunk and beat his wife up badly, leaving her covered with welts and bruises all over her legs and torso. He said that between the alcohol and the rage he was feeling, he went "berserk." However, when his counselors asked him why his wife didn't have injuries to her face or arms, he answered, "Oh, I wasn't going to do anything that would show."

We have seen relationship after relationship where a raging man does one of the following: "goes crazy", smashes things around the house, and yet manages to avoid breaking anything that is important to him (while he breaks lots of things of hers); behaves in ways that are "out of control" but then quickly covers his tracks when police come around so that they won't find out about the drugs or the violence or the drunk driving; is in the middle of being verbally and emotionally vicious to her when other people show up, and he switches so quickly to being kind and smiley that those people have no idea what she is so upset about, and she actually comes out looking like the nasty one.

If you are serious about changing, you have to be willing to look at the choices you are making every day, from the most trivial to the most significant. You need to accept that no one and nothing other than you is determining what you do. If you backslide into drinking, if you return to abusive behavior, if you cheat on your partner, it's because that's what you decided to do. In short:

Your change depends on your willingness to accept *complete responsibility* for your own actions. You have to stop blaming them on your partner, your addiction, your childhood, your feelings, or anything else.

Is mental illness a legitimate excuse for being abusive?

The truth is that only the most severe mental illnesses cause people to become truly unable to make choices or govern their own actions. If you can hold down a job, get along a lot of the time with your friends or relatives, and appear more or less normal in most situations, you are in adequate shape psychologically to be fully responsible for your actions.

The kind of mental health conditions that leave a man genuinely out of control are on the level of hearing voices and having visual hallucinations that seem completely real, remembering events that never happened, believing harmless people are trying to kill you, and confusing your worst nightmares with reality.

Very few people are dealing with psychological problems this severe; and even at this level of mental health crisis, the person's values and attitudes still influence their actions.

The more common mental health problems, such as depression, manic depression, and personality disorder, as serious as they can be, do not make it impossible for a person to make better choices if they become motivated to do so. The first step, then, is to acknowledge that you are making choices. Unhook yourself from the idea that everyone else is causing your suffering, and that you "just couldn't help" the destructive things you have done.

Brett, who has gone through two years of Dialectical Behavioral Therapy to deal with his borderline personality disorder, puts it this way: "I realize that I have never acted in any way that would seriously hurt my reputation at work. If I acted on all of the thoughts that went through my head, I would not only have lost my relationship, but also my job and everything I have. I would be homeless. I have a 'switch'—it's my ability to choose. I throw on that switch before I go to work and I can function really well. I finally realized that if I want to keep this relationship, I have to throw on that switch *at home.* "

Homework:

Write down the story of a time when you told yourself that you "lost control of yourself" and did something destructive. Looking back at that event, how can you tell now that you were actually making choices at the time? Why did you make the choices that you did?

Lesson 36: Owning The Harm You Have Caused

(Source: L. Bancroft, *Guide for Men Who Are Serious About Changing – Part 2*)

Meaningful behavioral change doesn't occur in people who lack the strength or the integrity to look squarely at the damage their actions have wrought. The pop philosophy that says, "Forget the past, just focus on doing better in the future" may work well for the baseball player who just missed a catch, but it fails disastrously in the hands of a destructive man. Why?

Because your failure to consider, value, and understand your partner's feelings is a central reason for why you behaved in such hurtful ways in the first place. You can't possibly move beyond selfishness and insensitivity unless you are willing to spend a long time — quite likely years — developing your understanding of how you have hurt your partner, and learning to care about that harm and repair it.

Another mistake in pop philosophy says; "guilt is a pointless emotion, and nothing is accomplished by feeling guilty about something you've done." In reality, guilt is a critical aspect of healthy human functioning. Our guilt feelings exist to alert us to times when we have wronged other people and to motivate us not to repeat those unethical or uncaring acts.

The definition of a psychopath is a person who lacks a conscience; in other words, a person who feels no guilt about having harmed another. ***The absence of guilt is a sign that something is deeply wrong.*** Usually, the nagging conscience we feel toward others is there for a good reason.

Do we want a man to feel guilty about embarrassing his wife because he got stumbling drunk in front of her relatives? About how humiliated she felt when he called her a "fat bitch"? About the years when he was stealing her money to buy cocaine? About bringing home a sexually transmitted disease because he was cheating on her?

Yes, we do. **Guilt is not an end in itself, but the only way for a man *not* to feel guilty about these kinds of behaviors is to not really look at them.** He has to force them out of his mind, minimize them, blame them on his partner, or blame them on women in general. And if he is going to change, we need him to look.

Part of why the alcoholic drinks is, ironically, to escape the pain of the damage that his drinking has already done. Part of why the abuser keeps abusing is to punish his partner for daring to point out how his abuse has hurt her. Part of why the man with narcissistic personality disorder behaves so selfishly is to try to fill a huge internal void he experiences, which in turn is caused by the fact that he has driven so many people away over the years. All that effort he pours into not seeing himself is cement being poured into the foundation of his problem.

You don't have to take our word for it. Twelve-step programs for recovery from addiction place emphasis on the importance of "taking a fearless moral inventory" of one's own acts, and doing the extended work of "making amends."

Programs for men who abuse women focus on requiring the men to grasp the effects of their violence and to learn to *feel bad* about treating a woman that way. Dialectical Behavioral Therapy, the state-of-the-art approach to overcoming personality disorders, demands that participants immediately stop behaving in ways that make things worse; then they work on the skills of preserving relationships by learning to consider the implications of their choices.

As Brett says; "when she's mad at me, I have to stop and think about my skills. I take a moment and ask myself, how do I want her to feel about me in twenty minutes? How do *I* want to feel later about this interaction? She's got every right to be pissed off at me. I have to remember everything I put her through""Thinking in that way goes against all the negative voices in my head—but those voices are going to get me divorced. And I want to be with her. I want her to trust me."

The Elements of Facing What You Have Done

- Be able to describe, in detail, the wrongs you have done.

- Be able to say a lot about how your behavior has affected your partner without making her sound hypersensitive, fragile, or over-reactive.

- Put these thoughts in writing and allow your partner to keep copies of what you have written.

- Give her as much space as she wants, for as long as she wants, to express her hurt, anger, frustration, and other feelings about your conduct, and to let you know what the other specific effects have been on her life (such as financial harm you have brought her, opportunities you have caused her to miss, ways you have harmed the children, physical injuries you have caused, lasting damage you have brought to her trust in you or to her sense of safety in the world).

- Do everything in your power to take care of the harm you have done (such as paying her medical or therapy bills, going back now to anyone you have lied to about her in the past and tell the truth, fixing harm you've done to the home, helping the children cope with emotional difficulties your behavior has sown in them, paying her back money you owe her or that you stole from her, getting a job and holding it down).

- Accept that there will be aspects of the harm you did that you *can't* fix, and that your partner has a right to express anger and bitterness for a long time about those effects.

This list is useful when you are sinking into feeling like, given all the damage you have done, it is too late to do anything good. But whether your relationship works out or not, you have the responsibility to do everything constructive that you can to make up for harm you have done. The list above gives you several ideas of what you can do. Taking every step you possibly can may not bring your partner back to you, but it will help her to heal emotionally, and will help you to regain your sense of decency and dignity in who you are.

Homework:

Do some extended writing (filling a few pages) about how your partner has been affected by your unhealthy behavior in the past. Make it honest, and face your actions bravely. Let her read it when you are finished *if she wishes to*. If she does read it, be prepared to listen non defensively to any reactions and additions she may have, or new pieces she wants you to write about.

Lesson 37: Stop Bargaining

(Source: L. Bancroft, *Guide for Men Who Are Serious About Changing – Part 2*)

Anyone who has unhealthy behavior patterns, whether it be alcohol abuse, cheating or other mistreatment of their partner, or chronic irresponsibility, gets attached to those behaviors. So when you start to work on change, you will inevitably face some internal battles, where part of you wants to stay on the new road and another part of you keeps an eye open for opportunities to go back to your familiar ways. One way you may do this is by trying to *cut deals* regarding your change, which might look like any of the following:

- Telling your partner that you have made big changes, and that it's unreasonable for her to expect you to change even more.

- Saying that your partner doesn't appreciate how hard you have been working on yourself.

- Acting as if a period of behaving appropriately gives you license to behave badly now (for example, you get drunk and then say to her; "but I've been on the wagon for a long time, you partner shouldn't be so mad, you don't appreciate how well I've been doing").

- Using your change as a bargaining chip to force your partner to do more to please you, such as; "I quit smoking weed like you wanted me to, so now you should quit hanging around with your sister so much, like I've wanted," or, "okay, I'll stop yelling and calling you names about how messy the house is, but then you've got to keep it cleaner".

- Managing your alcohol or drug problem by *bingeing,* where you don't use for weeks at a time but then you get yourself hammered enough in a weekend to make up for all the time of not partying.

Each of these bargains deserves a response. First of all, there is nothing unreasonable about your partner expecting you to completely stop your destructive behavior. In fact, you are the one being unreasonable by suggesting that your partner should be willing to endure any more of it. Does it make sense to say to her (in effect), "because I treated you so badly in the past, you should accept some mistreatment now, as long as it's less than it used to be"? Or, to put it even more starkly: "you can't complain if I steal a little of your money today, because I used to steal *a lot* of it"? Of course not.

We would, in fact, argue the opposite; we believe that the fact that you have behaved badly in the past gives you even *less* license to do so in the present, because your partner is already emotionally injured by you and you have no right to poke her in the wounded places.

Similarly, your partner doesn't owe you gratitude for treating her the way you should have treated her all along. If you want to congratulate yourself for how much you have changed, or if your friends want to give you a prize, that's great, but don't look for, or demand, credit from the person you have hurt. If someone is holding you on the ground with a foot on your neck—speaking metaphorically—you aren't going to thank them when they step off and let you get up.

Men with histories of irresponsible relationship behavior share this tendency to try to make bargains. The immature guy thinks he should be admired for finally working a steady job. The partier thinks we should be impressed that he finally stopped snorting coke and smoking weed. The abusive man wants us to shake his hand for not threatening his wife and calling her disgusting names. But good behavior, even if it continues for weeks or months, does not earn a man a gift certificate that he can then redeem for a day of acting like a selfish or scary jerk.

Nor does it earn you the right to control or change something you don't like about her, or to demand that she cater to you more, King of the Castle style. This style of bargaining is called "quid pro quo," which means that you are setting it up so that if your partner wants you to do something for her (such as meet your responsibilities, then she has to do something for you. It's important for you to gain clarity on this point:

When she insists that you be a good relationship partner, she's not asking you for a *favor;* she's asking for her *due.* You don't get to demand anything back from her in return for you being a decent and responsible human being.

Untangling this bargain leads us to another critical point to highlight:

You have to make your changes *unconditionally* or they absolutely will not last. You are changing *because it is the right thing to do,* and therefore it cannot be done with the expectation that she will do anything in return.

In fact, you may make what feels like big changes to you, and she may still decide to end the relationship. Again, the fact that you are doing better than you used to do does not confer any obligation on her — you should have been behaving right all along.

Bargaining is a warning sign of change that isn't happening. If you stop drinking because you think that will get your partner to go on a diet for you; or you stop calling your partner a slut but expect that in return she'll stop talking to her male friends; or you stop stealing her money but you feel that in return she should "help you out" by giving you money voluntarily, then your thinking isn't changing.

Lesson 38: Making Meaningful Apologies

(Source: L. Bancroft, *Guide for Men Who Are Serious About Changing – Part 2*)

"Why do I still have to be hearing about this? I already told you I was sorry! What more do you want from me, a pound of flesh?"

Does the person who makes the above statement sound like he's sorry? Not a bit. In fact, he is communicating the message that, whatever he's saying he apologized about, he actually doesn't at all see what was wrong with what he did. He just used that apology to placate his partner and get her to leave him alone.

Look through the following box:

The Characteristics Of A Meaningful Apology

You sound like you really mean it when you say it.

You make a serious commitment not to repeat the behavior.

Even after you apologize, you give your partner the time she needs to explain to you what was wrong with what you did and how your actions affected her.

You show signs over time of making a serious effort to grasp why your partner didn't like what you did.

You respect her right to have additional bad feelings about the event that come up later, especially when something triggers the experience for her.

You respect her right to demand that you *do something* about the acts you displayed..

The Characteristics of a Useless Apology

You insist that your apology should be all your partner need from you.

You blame her for not feeling finished with the event, insisting that it's her job to put it all behind her.

You don't back up the apology with much action.

You keep doing the same things over and over again and then apologizing again.

You switch into the victim role if your partner remains angry or mistrustful about something you did, and you make it sound like she's being mean or unfair to you about it.

You act annoyed if she points out that your apology didn't sound heartfelt.

You make a hurried or unfeeling apology, or you retract it later.

Let's consider an example. Maryellen is having a difficult pregnancy and the doctor tells her that it's essential that she get some exercise. She and her husband, Luke, agree that three days a week he is going to hurry home from work to look after their two children while she goes to the gym. But only the second day into this agreement, Luke gets offered some high-paying overtime and accepts it (without asking Maryellen), so she remains trapped in the house all evening. Maryellen expresses her fury to Luke when he finally gets home, and he ends up apologizing before they go to bed. Two weeks later Maryellen says something to Luke about feeling under stress about their financial situation, and he snarls; "well, we wouldn't be in this position if you wouldn't have a fit about me getting in some overtime!"

Luke's comment is a *retraction* of his earlier apology (though he may deny that); he's now saying she shouldn't have been upset by what he did. He has just demonstrated, also, that he never did bother to think carefully about her needs and feelings (or the needs of their growing baby), and instead stayed mentally locked onto himself. Luke has switched the issue from being about Maryellen's need to exercise, and his need to honor his agreements, to being about her "having a fit." He has revealed that his original apology had nothing behind it.

Accepting Her Anger

A succinct way to summarize Luke's thinking is: "Maryellen has no right to be angry at me. Her anger is ridiculous. I'm going to put her down about it." One of the most consistent characteristics of men with unhealthy relationship patterns is that they dismiss and discredit the anger that their actions have caused. This discrediting tendency is sometimes worsened by a man's negative attitude toward women's anger in general; he may be contemptuous of women when they are angry, perhaps making demeaning imitations of them or making them sound irrational and hysterical.

Therefore, one of the central pieces of work you have to do is to learn to respect, reflect upon, and respond appropriately to your partner's anger and to women's anger in general.

Homework:

Write your partner a thoughtful, detailed letter of apology about one of the hurts you have done to her that she has complained about the most. Follow the elements above of what makes a meaningful apology, including writing out your commitments regarding what you will do differently in the future. Then, follow through on this commitment in the months and years to come. Give her the letter *if she is interested in having it.* Accept any reactions she has to the letter, including accepting her right not to react at all.

Lesson 39: Destructive Beliefs About Manhood

(Source: L. Bancroft, *Guide For Men Who Are Serious About Changing – Part 2*)

Sooner or later, a man who is interested in becoming a responsible, kind, sober partner is going to find himself struggling with insecurities about his manhood. As part of that process, he is going to have to come to terms with the mixed messages he has absorbed about masculinity over the course of his life, beginning when he was very young. We find that men's unhealthy behavior patterns are highly connected to their gender identity, whether that plays out in obvious ways—as with men who batter their partners because they don't believe women have any rights—or plays out in much subtler ways, as with the man who won't stop drinking because he feels that without partying with his buddies he will lose his status as "one of the guys."

Our society's messages about manhood include some powerful binds that leave almost every man feeling that he isn't man enough:

- He is taught that he should be a good provider and a responsible family man BUT he also learns that he should value his male friends more than women and children, and spend his free time with them.

- He knows that he is supposed to be the strongest and the bravest BUT in reality only one man can be the strongest and the bravest, so that leaves all other men not quite up to snuff.

- He hears that he should be able to "handle his liquor" (which means he should be able to drink a lot) BUT he also gets the message that he shouldn't drink too much and especially that he should avoid the shame of being an alcoholic.

- He learns that he should not open up about his feelings or "show weakness" emotionally, BUT his pain sometimes, (or frequently) becomes more than he can endure.

- He learns that a man should never back down from a fight BUT he also learns that he's supposed to keep his family safe, and his aggressive behavior can endanger his whole family.

- He learns that a real man has to have lots of money, power and women BUT his efforts in that direction are leading him to hypertension, drug or alcohol addiction, illegal behavior (such as drug dealing, embezzlement, or taking bribes), and cheating on his partner.

- He learns that men are intellectually superior to women and shouldn't take women seriously BUT without accepting substantial leadership and guidance from women—including his partner—he's never going to turn his life around.

Many positive, constructive messages about what it means to be a man are also part of a male's socialization, but they get interwoven with pro-violence and anti-female training (see the box below). Your capacity for change will expand greatly if you take on the project of untangling this knot inside of yourself.

MESSAGES ABOUT MASCULINITY

Healthy	Unhealthy
Men should be courageous. They should fight for what they believe in and fight to protect those whom they love	Men should never be afraid. They should never back down from a threat or challenge.
Men should be tough, and be prepared to endure hardship for the good of their loved ones and their communities.	Men should be unfeeling and unemotional, and especially should not cry.
Men should be protective of those they love.	Men should view women as weak and incapable of protecting themselves.
Men should be good providers for their families.	Men should have the privileged position and should receive the best (best food, best leisure, best "toys," above the rest of his family.
Men should treat women with respect.	Men should control women, look upon them as lesser beings; use them for sex.
Men should be good, loving fathers.	Men should be the disciplinarians and should toughen up their children.
Men should be proud.	Men should ruin their own pride with shameful or dictatorial behavior (e.g. drunkenness, violence toward women and children,) which undermines their own dignity.
Men should be prepared to make sacrifices so their families and communities can benefit.	Men should expect their family and communities to sacrifice for them.

Looking at the surface, you might think, "What do a man's internal conflicts about masculinity have to do with smoking weed, or calling names in an argument, or having a mental health problem?" But closer examination inevitably reveals that the contradictions above are playing a role. In order to come through as a loving and responsible partner, it is necessary to work through these societal pressures and build a healthy definition of what it means to be a "real man".

Homework:

Spend some time writing about what you think a "real man" is like, and how such a man should live. Which messages have you been taught about manhood that you believe are good ones to follow? What unhealthy messages have you been taught? Which men in your life should you spend less time with because they promote an unhealthy version of masculinity? What men are better role models for you? What women in your life should you open yourself up to accept more influence from?

Next, look back through the box above. You will find that you were taught each of these beliefs, even though the ones on the right contradict the ones on the left. Consider where each of these messages, both the good ones and the bad ones, came into your life from. Your father or stepfather? Male relatives? Your friends? Your faith community? Television shows? Popular songs? Sayings?

Lesson 40: Developing Skills For Regulating Your Emotional States

(Source: L. Bancroft, *Guide For Men Who Are Serious About Changing – Part 2*)

It's typical for people with mental health difficulties or a history of trauma, commonly to have serious difficulties with managing the emotional stresses of daily life. Small frustrations or setbacks can feel huge and unbearable. They may cycle, within a period of just a few hours, between elation, depression, rage, withdrawal, and hysterical laughter. If you live in the center of this kind of emotional tempest, you are no doubt exhausting both yourself and your partner. Moreover, in this kind of whirlwind you can't achieve the kind of internal calm necessary to do the hard work involved in transforming behavioral patterns.

Mental health problems also often cause internal splits, so that the different parts of a person are not integrated. The sense of internal division can contribute to erratic behavior, self-hatred, and high anxiety.

Given these challenges, learning better emotional self-regulation is key- it helps you reduce stress and anxiety, clears your head so you make better choices, and forms a consistent center to yourself.

You are much more likely to make significant progress in this arena if you seek out high-quality professional help. If possible, find a therapist trained in Cognitive Behavioral Therapy, "emotional regulation," or "distress tolerance." If you have no way to pay for this kind of assistance, or if it is not available close enough to where you live, work with the book *Don't Let Your Emotions Run Your Life* by S. Spradlin.

The skills that you need to work on developing include:

- Mindfulness (the ability to stay present and aware of what is going on around you even when you are upset).

- Methods to calm yourself (for example, to go off alone for a few minutes and settle yourself back down) rather than cranking yourself up more and more when you are upset.

- Strategies to better focus on the other person's perspective in an argument (rather than just "freaking out" and trying to rip their perspective to shreds).

- Meditation.

- Body awareness and integration techniques (such as yoga, watching your own breathing, and many others) to help you tune into your physiological processes and reactions.

- Healthy emotional releases, such as deep and prolonged crying.

A key point here is that your complaints about your partner can't be excuses for you to fly off the handle. Even at times when you have a justifiable reason to be angry at her or feel hurt by something she has done, you still must take the proper steps of:

(1) Bringing yourself back to center emotionally, and then,

(2) Raising your complaint with your partner in a reasonable way that doesn't involve screaming and doesn't communicate hatred or contempt.

If your partner is willing, establish an agreement with her regarding how you two are going to proceed when you "lose it" emotionally. For example, you might have an agreement that anytime she can see that you are turning dysregulated and irrational, you will walk off and be alone for ten minutes, and come back when you have pulled yourself together. (Remember, an agreement of this kind should also include an agreement about what you will do if you break the agreement, such as refuse to leave the room when she tells you that you are going off the deep end and need to take a break).

Replacing Destructive Attitudes with Positive Ones

Since emotional difficulty does not automatically lead to bad behavior—many people with mental health problems or trauma histories treat other people with kindness, avoid abusing substances, and maintain a honest, ethical behavior—it also follows that emotional healing does not lead directly to good behavior. Attitudes play an important role in contributing to men's problems with alcohol or drugs, immaturity, and mental health problems, and are the outstanding causes in men who are abusiveness.

When your partner puts you under pressure to deal with your issues, you may give in and say; "okay, I'll open up more about my emotions and inner struggles." This is a promising step. However, this step won't help if you use it as an excuse to focus exclusively on your feelings and avoid looking at, and reforming, your ways of *thinking*. You will need to keep turning your energy toward changing your values and beliefs, including your way of viewing your partner. **Attitudinal change is indispensable; without it, no other improvements will last.**

Refer to the following list to guide you in transforming your internal messages:

- "I lose control of myself, I'm helpless"NEEDS TO BECOME:"my behavior is a choice that I make."

- "My partner is a bitch"NEEDS TO BECOME:"my partner is a human being worthy of respect 24/7."

- "She expects too much from me"NEEDS TO BECOME:"I need to meet my responsibilities."

- "I can't stand this"NEEDS TO BECOME:"these are the kinds of challenges everybody has to deal with."

- "Looking after the kids is a burden"NEEDS TO BECOME:"I'm so lucky to have this time with our children."

- "Look at all my partner's faults"NEEDS TO BECOME:"I'm going to focus on what I appreciate about her."

- "She owes it to me to have sex with me"NEEDS TO BECOME: "intimacy is never her obligation" and "my history of behavior hasn't exactly been a turn-on for her."

- "She shouldn't be so upset with me"NEEDS TO BECOME:"I'm lucky she's still willing to give this relationship a chance, given how I've been."

If your partner feels motivated to write a list for you of what she feels your most chronically unhealthy attitudes have been, accept it, and consider it a gift she's giving you toward turning your life around. If she's willing to provide you with such a list, you should work with it by looking at each attitude she wrote for you, and then write down next to it what the corresponding proper outlook would be for each of the items your partner gave you (drawing some ideas from the "Needs to Become" list above).

Then go on to the exercise below.

Homework:

First, make a list of the destructive attitudes you have had in the following categories:

1. Reasons you tell yourself why you are helpless about your own behavior.

2. Reasons why you have to drink or drug, or why no one should ask you not to.

3. Negative views of your partner, including unfair demands and expectations you have had about her.

4. Reasons why the world is responsible for your difficulties.

Next to each item you write down, put a new, positive attitude to take instead.

Second, monitor your own thinking over the weeks ahead, and when you notice a destructive attitude, write it down, and put the corresponding healthy attitude next to it.

Note well that this exercise will rapidly become counterproductive if you use it as an excuse to catalog your partner's faults, feel sorry for yourself, or be sarcastic. Do this exercise as a sincere effort to look at yourself or don't do it at all.

Lesson 41: Be Serious About Changing

(Source: L. Bancroft, *Guide For Men Who Are Serious About Changing – Part 2*)

Honoring your promises and commitments is a centerpiece of building the new you. So if you told your partner you were going to take important steps, but now you are coming up with excuses not to go through with them, notice that and get back to work, with no whining allowed. Are you slipping into any of the following indications of backsliding?

- Did you say you were willing to go to therapy, but over time you have started to make more and more excuses for skipping; such as complaining about the money or saying the therapist isn't that good?

- Did you say you would get a sponsor in AA but you haven't, or you did get one but you aren't carrying the ball on speaking regularly with him or her?

- Did you agree initially to sign up for an abuser intervention program, but now you're starting to say that you don't really have time for that, or that you think you can manage your behavior without the program?

- Were you looking into using trauma services, but now you're saying you can heal on your own?

Our message here is simple: **you have to follow through on getting proper help for yourself**, and without your partner dragging you, kicking and screaming each step of the way. If you could grow on your own, you would have done so years ago. Learning how to find and accept appropriate help is part of maturing (and it differs from whining and demanding help from your partner).

No one **changes from chronic unhealthy behaviors, or heals from serious trauma, alone.** If you have shame about needing assistance, that is a normal reaction, but you can't let it stop you. Promises that aren't backed up by concrete action go nowhere.

And if it happens that you need to switch therapists, or change sponsors, or make some other adjustment to the plan you made (back in Chapter 1), it is critical to follow these steps:

1) Work out a new plan that your partner is comfortable with, and

2) *Follow your old plan until the new one is in place.* In other words, you can't quit therapy while you find a new therapist, and you can't skip talking to your sponsor while you choose another sponsor.

We have many times watched a man with destructive patterns backs off from his plan for outside help, start to not keep certain other aspects of his agreements, and then fall back completely into his unhealthy — and often self-destructive behavior. This is the most slippery of slopes. Any time you catch yourself doing this kind of "I can handle this alone" thinking, recognize that as one of the symptoms of your problem and snap out of it.

Developing, And Keeping To A Daily Practice

Because your unhealthy habits have come to feel familiar and natural to you, your change process is akin to turning someone who rarely exercises into a fit competitive athlete; you will have to work at change and growth *every day of the week* or you will not progress. Your recovery program should be in writing and be posted on the wall in a place where you can see it easily, and should specify which actions you will take on which day of the week. Depending on what your patterns have been, the program will include such elements as:

- Making the decision each morning that you will not drink that day.

- Reading a set number of pages from a book you are working through, and writing some thoughts about what you read.

- Calling your sponsor.

- Attending a meeting.

- Giving your partner at least three thoughtful appreciations during the day.

- Meeting specific household and child-care responsibilities.

- Thinking each morning about how you will, for that day, replace abusive attitudes you have had toward your partner with respectful ones.

- Attending an individual or group therapy session.

- Meditating.

- Attending your abuser program.

There are other daily commitments that your plan might include, based on what your core issues and chronic behaviors have been. Some items might appear on your schedule every day of the week, while others (such as attending therapy or a support group) might be one or more times per week on specified days.

Brett describes his practice in this way: "Every day before I get out of bed I say to myself, 'I have a personality disorder.' I'm not putting myself down; I'm just getting it straight. Otherwise, I get back into really distorted thinking. I know it isn't my fault that I got this way, but it's my responsibility to keep my head clear and not keep being selfish or mean."

Lesson 42: Grief Recovery: Lesson 1

(Source: *The Grief Recovery Handbook*, by James& Friedman)

The purpose of this handout is to learn how to **complete** your grief and recovery rather than participating in *isolation* and *avoidance.*

Grief is the conflicting feelings caused by the end of or change in a familiar pattern of behavior. Examples of conflicting feelings are *relief* and *pain*.

There is a difference between grief and grief recovery. The purpose of this class is to experience **grief recovery**.

Recovery from loss is achieved by a series of small and correct choices made by the griever.

The way to experience grief recovery is to **complete your grief**.

General truths regarding grief:

- The defining stages of grief are not always helpful.

- There are some common responses to grief:

    o Reduced concentration

    o A sense of numbness

    o Disrupted sleep patterns

    o Changed eating patterns

    o Roller coaster emotional energy

- All relationships are unique. There is no "one size fits all" to grieving.

- Unhelpful words for grievers: denial, closure, guilt, survivor.

Remember: There is nothing wrong with you.

We are all unprepared to deal with loss. We are taught to acquire things, not to lose them.

Common myths people are taught about grief:

1. Don't feel bad.

2. Replace the loss.

3. Grieve alone.

4. Just give it time.

5. Be strong for others.

6. Keep Busy.

Homework/Writing Assignment: Write about any of these above myths that you can relate to. Add any other ideas that you were taught or have observed in those around you in connection to loss events.

Write about any of the following common comments that you may have heard in connection to loss:

"Get a hold of yourself".

"You can't fall apart".

"Keep a stiff upper lip".

"Pull yourself up by your bootstraps".

"We understand how you feel".

"Be thankful you have other children".

"The living must go on".

"He's in a better place".

"All things must pass".

"She led a full life".

"God will never give you more than you can handle".

Review the above list and add some comments of your own that you may have heard or even said throughout your life. Write thoroughly about how these myths and ideas have affected your ability to process your grief.

Lesson 43: Grief Recovery The Healthy Way

(Source: *The Grief Recovery Handbook*, by James & Friedman)

Acting Recovered:

In general, our society teaches us to **act recovered**. A false image of recovery is the most common obstacle all grievers must overcome if they expect to move beyond their loss.

So often, grievers find themselves simply saying, "I'm fine." The problem with saying, "I'm fine," is that it does not help the broken heart. This saying merely distracts both the griever and others, while the pain and loneliness of the loss still remain inside. The net effect is to create a scab over an infection.

Unresolved grief leaves the griever feeling:

- A massive loss of energy

- A loss of aliveness

    o This experience occurs when people have a "false recovery" based on their own convincing performance.

    o Every time a loss is not properly concluded, there is a cumulative restriction on our aliveness.

Being Realistic:

Having a realistic view of the person you lost:

- **Idolize** – One attempt to look recovered is to focus only on the fond memories of the person who has died. This does not allow the griever to look accurately at all aspects of the relationship.

- **Villainize** – This is the opposite of idolizing the lost person. The griever may have a litany of complaints detailing a lifetime of mistreatment. He/she is often unwilling to let go of disappointment and anger.

It is almost impossible to complete the pain caused by a loss without looking at everything about the relationship, not just the positive or the negative.

All relationships include both positive and negative interactions. We know that you can complete grief only by being totally honest with yourself and others.

Homework/Writing Assignment: Please think about and write out your answers to the following questions.

How have you and do you "act" recovered?

In what ways do you idolize your lost loved one?

In what ways do you villainize your lost loved one?

Analyze your need for the approval of others. How do you need the approval of others?

Who is Responsible?

- It is important to learn to take responsibility for our own feelings.

- Beware that we can develop a victim mentality when we believe that others have the power to make us feel certain ways.

- Eleanor Roosevelt: *"No one can make you feel bad about yourself without your permission."*

- When we give the responsibility of our feelings to other people, we also give them responsibility for ending our feelings.

- Realize in large part that your feelings result from your attitudes and actions.

What ruins the picnic – the rain or one's attitude about the rain? The answer is both. The rain really does ruin the picnic, but you cannot do anything about the rain, you can only deal with your reaction to the rain.

We must take responsibility for our current reaction to what happened to us in the past; otherwise, we will forever feel like victims.

Nothing can change until you take responsibility for your own recovery.

To heal from grief, be willing to take the responsibility for your part of what is not complete – even if it is only 1 percent your responsibility. Work with that 1 percent.

Questions:

Have you ever struggled with giving responsibility of your feelings to others?

If so, how have you disowned your responsibility for your feelings?

Lesson 44: Grief Recovery: The Relationship Graph

"Truth is the key to recovery."

(Source: *The Grief Recovery Handbook*, by James& Friedman)

Draw a relationship graph showing a time line of the relationship from beginning to now. Draw a horizontal line across your paper and then draw vertical lines above the line that are positive experiences and draw vertical lines below the lines to show the negative parts of your relationship. Once you are done with the line, look at it and complete the following exercises.

The point of the Relationship Graph is to take a complete and detailed look at one relationship. At some point after a loss occurs, your brain begins a review, searching for what was never communicated or completed. The purpose of this assignment is to help you discover what is unfinished for you in your loss so that you can complete your grief. Successful completion of unfinished emotions allows you to become complete with the often painful reality that the physical relationship has ended.

Death is never a singular event. In addition to the actual death, there is the death of all the *hopes*, dreams, and expectations about the future.

Choose one relationship to focus on. The three aspects of the relationship that you will focus on in this assignment are: (a) Physical, (b) Emotional, (c) Spiritual

Remember, you can only complete your loss by acknowledging the truth. In order to effectively complete this process, you must be totally honest with *yourself* in relation to others.

Use a sheet of paper of at least 8.5" x 11." Turn the paper sideways and draw a line from left to right across the middle of the page. The left end represents the beginning of the relationship. The right end of the line represents the present.

Relationships do not end with death or divorce. The emotional aspects of the relationship continue in your memory even after death or divorce has happened. Positive or happy events are marked above the center line, and negative or sad events below the line.

The following are a list of points to consider as you draw your relationship graph:

- Go to the beginning and reconstruct the relationship to the best of your ability.

- Let your mind wander. Do not edit or limit; rather, recall and note.

- Honesty and thoroughness are essential.

- Do not judge what happened. Do not intellectualize, focus on your feelings.

- Try to maintain truth and accuracy and avoid enshrinement or villainizing.

- Do not fall in to the trap that the relationship was all good or all bad. Be realistic.

- Your goal is to identify the undelivered communications.

- Think about what you wish were *different*, *better*, or *more*, as well as *unrealized hopes*, *dreams*, and *expectations* about the future.

- What do you wish you would have said or not said?

- What do you wish you would have done or not done?

- What do you wish the other person had said or not said?

- What do you wish the other person had not said or not done?

Give yourself about an hour to complete this assignment. Next: share with a listening partner and bring back to group for discussion.

Lesson 45: Grief Recovery: The Relationship Graph
Part 2

Now it is time to translate your Relationship Graph into recovery components:

- Apologies

- Forgiveness

- Significant Emotional Statements

Now take out your Relationship Graph. Go through it one event at a time and assign a recovery category to each event. Generally, above-the-line events will be either apologies or significant emotional statements. Below-the-line events will be either forgiveness or significant emotional statements. Some events will require two categories.

Apologies:

You make apologies for anything you did or did not do that might have hurt someone else.

Note: Victims have difficulty with apologies. Some people develop lifelong relationships with their pain and feel like victims. This often becomes a life-limiting and restricting habit. When in this mindset, people often have a hard time apologizing. In spite of this reality, there is a need to apologize for your transgressions no matter how slight they may be.

Sometimes our desire to be right can be a big problem in making apologies. Our sense of justice and self-righteousness can keep us stuck. Because the other person has harmed us, we forget that we aren't perfect.

Since this exercise involves a loss, you will most likely need to apologize to your loved one indirectly. The objective is to complete your hurt and grief. To do this, be totally honest with yourself and allow yourself to apologize for anything harmful you did in the relationship with your lost loved one.

Forgiveness:

Forgiveness is giving up the hope of a different or better yesterday.

It is important to distinguish the word *forgive* from the word *condone*:

- Forgive: "to cease to feel resentment against an offender.

- Condone: "to treat as if trivial, harmless, or of no importance."

Successful grief recovery requires completion of the pain rather than retention of the resentment.

Here are some statements to say to help you take the action of forgiveness:

"I acknowledge the things that you did or did not do that hurt me, and I am not going to let them hurt me anymore."

r, *"I acknowledge the things that you did or did not do that hurt me, and I'm not going to let my memory of those incidents hurt me anymore."*

Remember, *forgiveness has very little to do with the other person.* You cannot feel forgiveness until you do it. A feeling of forgiveness can result only from the action of verbalizing the forgiveness.

Actions first, feelings follow

It is also important to remember *not to forgive a person directly to his/her face.* The person being forgiven need not know that it has ever happened.

The exercise in forgiveness is to help you heal; it is for your recovery, not the other person.

Significant Emotional Statements:

Any undelivered emotional communication that is neither an apology nor a forgiveness conveniently falls into the catchall category of significant emotional statements.

It is the accumulation of a lifetime of unsaid things that contributes to a sense of incompleteness. Think of things that you wish had been *better* or *different* in the relationship.

Think of things you wish you would have said or done, or hadn't said or done.

When a relationship ends there is often the realization of a sense of broken *hopes*, *dreams*, and *expectations*.

Now is the time to put words on the thoughts and feelings that the loss robbed you of the opportunity to communicate.

Lesson 46: Personal Accountability

Written by: Kai Cheng Thom

1. Listen to the Survivor

When you have been abusive it is very essential to learn how to listen to the person you have hurt. Here are some essential ingredients for listening to someone you have harmed:

- Listen without becoming defensive.

- Listen without trying to equivocate or make excuses.

- Listen without minimizing or denying the extent of the harm.

- Listen without trying to make yourself the center of the story being told.

When someone, particularly a partner or loved one, tells you that you have hurt or abused them, it can be easy to understand this as an accusation or attack. Very often, this is our first assumption – that we are being attacked.

This is why so many perpetrators of abuse respond to survivors who confront them by saying something along the lines of; "I'm not abusing you. You are abusing me, right now, with this accusation!"

But this is the cycle of violence talking. This is the script that rape culture has built for us: a script in which there must be a hero and a villain, a right and a wrong, an accuser and an accused.

What if we understood being confronted about perpetuating abuse as an act of courage – even a gift – on the part of the survivor?

What if, instead of reacting immediately in our own defense, we instead took the time to listen, to really try to understand the harm we might have done to another person?

When we think of accountability in terms of listening and love instead of accusation and punishment, everything changes.

2. Take responsibility for the abuse

After listening, the next step in holding one's self accountable is taking responsibility for the abuse. This means, simply enough; agreeing that you *and only you* are the source of physical, emotional, or psychological violence directed toward another person.

A simple analogy for taking responsibility for abuse can be made to taking responsibility for stepping on someone else's foot: There are many reasons why you might do such a thing – you were in a hurry, you weren't looking where you were going, or maybe no one ever taught you that it was wrong to step on other people's feet.

But you still did it. No one else – only you are responsible, and it is up to you to acknowledge and apologize for it.

The same holds true for abuse: no one, and I really mean *no one* – not your partner, not patriarchy, not mental illness, not society, not the Devil – is responsible for the violence that you do to another person.

A lot of factors can *contribute* to or influence one's reasons for committing abuse (see the point below), but in the end, only I, am responsible for my actions, as you are for yours.

3. Accept that your reasons are not excuses

There is an awful, pervasive myth out there that people who abuse others do so simply because they are bad people – because they are sadistic, or because they enjoy other people's pain.

This is, I think, part of the reason why so many people who have been abusive in the past or present resist the use of the terms "abuse" or "abuser" to describe their behavior. In fact, very, very, *very* few people who abuse are motivated to do so by sadism.

In my experience as a therapist and community support worker, when people are abusive, it's usually because they have a reason based in desperation or suffering.

Some reasons for abusive behavior I have heard include:

I am isolated and alone, and the only person who keeps me alive is my partner. This is why I can't let my partner leave me.

My partner hurts me all the time. I was just hurting them back.

I am sick, and if I don't force people to take care of me, then I will be left to die.

I am suffering, and the only way to relieve the pain is to hurt myself or others.

I didn't know that what I was doing was abuse. People always did the same to me. I was just following the script.

No one will love me unless I make them.

All of these are powerful, real reasons for abuse – but they are also *never* excuses. There is no reason good enough to excuse abusive behavior.

Reasons help us understand abuse, but they do not excuse it.

Accepting this is essential to transforming culpability into accountability and turning justice into healing.

4. Don't play the "Survivor Olympics"

As I mentioned above, communities tend to operate on a survivor/abuser or victim/perpetrator dichotomy model of abuse. This is the belief that people who have survived abuse in one relationship can never be abusive in other relationships.

I find that social justice or leftist communities also tend to misapply social analysis to individual situations of abuse, suggesting that individuals who belong to oppressed or marginalized groups can never abuse individuals who belong to privileged groups (that is, that women can never abuse men, racialized people can never abuse white people, and so on).

But neither of the above ideas is true. Survivors of abuse in one relationship can, in fact, be abusive in other relationships.

And it's for privileged individuals to abuse others because of the extra power social privilege gives them, but *anyone* is capable of abusing *anyone* given the right (or rather, wrong) circumstances.

It can be easy, when confronted with the abuse we have perpetrated, to try and play "Survivor Olympics."

"I can't be abusive," we may want to argue; "I'm a survivor!" Or "the abuse I have survived is so much worse than what you're accusing me of!" Or "nothing I do is abusive to you, because you have more privilege than me."

But survivors can be abusers, too.

Anyone can be abusive and comparing or trivializing doesn't absolve us of responsibility for it.

5. Take the survivor's lead

When having a dialogue with someone who has abused, it's essential to give the survivor the space to take the lead on expressing their needs and setting boundaries.

If you have abused someone, it's not up to you to decide how the process of healing or accountability should work.

Instead, it might be a good idea to try asking the person who has confronted you questions like: what do you need right now? Is there anything I can do to make this feel better? How much contact would you like to have with me going forward? If we share a community, how should I navigate situations where we might end up in the same place? How does this conversation feel for you, right now?

At the same time, it's important to understand that the needs of survivors of abuse can change over time, and that survivors may not always know right away – or ever – what their needs are.

Being accountable and responsible for abuse means being patient, flexible, and reflective with regards to the process of having dialogue with the survivor.

6. Face the fear of accountability

Being accountable for abuse takes a *lot* of courage.

We live in a culture that demonizes and oversimplifies abuse, probably because we don't want to accept the reality that abuse is actually commonplace and can be perpetrated by anybody.

A lot of people paint themselves into corners denying abuse, because, to be quite honest, it's terrifying to face the consequences, real and imagined, of taking responsibility.

And there are real risks: People have lost friends, communities, jobs, and resources over abuse. The risks are especially high for marginalized individuals – I am thinking particularly of Black and Brown folks here – who are likely to face harsh, discriminatory sentencing in legal processes.

There is nothing I can say to make this hard reality easier.

I can only suggest that when it comes to ending abuse, it's easier to face our fear than live in it all of our lives. It's more healing to tell the truth than to hide inside a lie.

When we hold ourselves accountable, we prove that the myth of the "monster" abuser is a lie.

7. Separate guilt from shame

Shame and social stigma are powerful emotional forces that can prevent us from holding ourselves accountable for being abusive: we don't want to admit to "being that person", so we don't admit to having been abusive at all.

Some people might suggest that people who have been abusive ought to feel shame – after all, perpetrating abuse is wrong. I would argue, though, that this is where the difference between guilt and shame is key:

Guilt is feeling bad about something you've done. Shame is feeling bad about who you are.

People who have been abusive should feel guilty – guilty for the specific acts of abuse they are responsible for. They should not feel shame about who they are, because this means that abuse has become a part of their identity.

It means that they believe that they are fundamentally a bad person – in other words, "an abuser."

But if you believe that you are an "abuser", a bad person who hurts others, then you have already lost the struggle for change – because we cannot change who we are.

If you believe that you are a fundamentally good person who has done hurtful or abusive things, then you open the possibility for change.

8. Don't expect anyone to forgive you

Being accountable is not fundamentally about earning forgiveness. That is to say, it doesn't matter how accountable you are – nobody has to forgive you for being abusive, least of all the person you have abused.

In fact, using the process of "doing" accountability to try and manipulate or coerce someone into giving their forgiveness to you is an extension of the abuse dynamic. It centers the abuser, not the survivor.

One shouldn't try to aim for forgiveness when holding oneself accountable. Rather, self-accountability is about learning how we have harmed others, why we have harmed others, and how we can stop.

But…

9. Forgive yourself

You do have to forgive yourself. Because you can't stop hurting other people until you stop hurting yourself.

When one is abusive, when one is hurting so much on the inside, that it feels like the only way to make it stop is to hurt other people, it can be terrifying to face the hard truth of words like *abuse* and *accountability*. One might rather blame others, blame society, blame the people we love, instead of ourselves.

This is true, I think, of community as well as individuals. It is so much easier, so much simpler, to create hard lines between good and bad people, to create walls to shut the shadowy archetype of "the abuser" out instead of mirrors to look at the abuser within.

Perhaps this is why self-accountability tools like this list are so rare.

It takes courage to be accountable. To decide to heal.

But when we do decide, we discover incredible new possibilities: there is good in everyone. Anyone is capable of change. And you are braver than you know.

Lesson 47: Cultural Issues: Who Is Affected By Domestic Violence?

Excerpted from: Delaware Coalition Against Domestic Violence

With one in four women victimized by domestic violence in her lifetime, each of us knows someone who has been affected, whether we know it or not. The survivor may be a family member, a coworker, someone who worships with you, a friend, or an acquaintance.

Domestic violence occurs in every culture, country, and age group. It affects people from all socioeconomic, educational, and religious backgrounds and happens in both same-sex and heterosexual relationships. Children are also affected by domestic violence, even if they are not abused or do not witness it directly.

The majority of victims of domestic violence are women, although men can also be victimized. According to the U.S. Department of Justice, women are 90-95 percent more likely to be victims of domestic violence than are men. Those men who are victimized include both men who experience intimate partner violence in gay relationships and men who are battered by a female partner.

Women with fewer resources or greater perceived vulnerability, including girls and those experiencing physical or psychiatric disabilities or living below the poverty line, are at the greatest risk for domestic violence and lifetime abuse.

Here are examples of how specific constituencies have been affected by domestic violence.

Teens

Teens – with technology at their fingertips – are increasingly vulnerable to dating-violence.

Approximately one in three adolescent girls in the United States is a victim of physical, emotional or verbal abuse from a dating partner – a figure that exceeds victimization rates for other types of violence affecting youth.

One in five tweens – ages 11to14 – say their friends are victims of dating violence, and nearly half who are in relationships know friends who are verbally abused. Two in five of the youngest teens, ages 11 and 12, report that their friends are victims of verbal abuse in relationships.

Teen victims of physical dating violence are more likely than their non-abused peers to smoke, use drugs, engage in unhealthy diet behaviors (taking diet pills or laxatives and vomiting to lose weight), engage in risky sexual behaviors, or attempt or consider suicide.

Technology has become a quick and easy way for stalkers to monitor and harass their victims. More than one in four stalking victims reports that some form of cyberstalking was used against them, such as e-mail (83% of all cyberstalking victims) or instant messaging (35%). More and more teens are using these communication vehicles to stay in touch with one another.

Dating Issues for Teenagers

Young adult dating violence is a big problem, affecting youth in every community across the nation. Learn the facts below.

This problem is too common

- Nearly 1.5 million high school students nationwide experience physical abuse from a dating partner in a single year.

- One in three adolescents in the U.S. is a victim of physical, sexual, emotional or verbal abuse from a dating partner, afigure that far exceeds rates of other types of youth violence.

- One in 10 high school students has been purposefully hit, slapped or physically hurt by a boyfriend or girlfriend.

- One quarter of high school girls have been victims of physical or sexual abuse.

- Girls and young women between the ages of 16 and 24 experience the highest rate of intimate partner violence --almost triple the national average.

- Violent behavior typically begins between the ages of 12 and 18.

- The severity of intimate partner violence is often greater in cases where the pattern of abuse was established in adolescence.

- About 72% of eighth and ninth graders are "dating".

Long-lasting Effects

Violent relationships in adolescence can have serious ramifications by putting the victims at higher risk for substanceabuse, eating disorders, risky sexual behavior and further domestic violence.

Being physically or sexually abused makes teen girls 6x more likely to become pregnant and twice as likely to get an STI.

Half of youth who have been victims of both dating violence and rape attempt suicide, compared to 12.5% of non-abusedgirls and 5.4% of non-abused boys.

Dating Violence And The Law

Eight states currently do not include dating relationships in their definition of domestic violence. As a result, youngvictims of dating abuse often cannot apply for restraining orders.

• New Hampshire is the only state where the law specifically allows a minor of any age to apply for a protection order; more than half of states do not specify the minimum age of a petitioner.

• Currently only one juvenile domestic violence court in the country focuses exclusively on teen dating violence.

Lack of Awareness

- Only 33% of teens who were in a violent relationship ever told anyone about the abuse.

- Eighty one percent of parents believe teen dating violence is not an issue or admit they don't know if it's an issue.

- A teen's confusion about the law and their desire for confidentiality are two of the most significant barriers stopping young victims of abuse from seeking help.

Immigrant Communities

Fear is the driving force behind many immigrants' reluctance to report acts of domestic violence to the authorities.

Reporting crimes and domestic violence to police or authorities generates fear of deportation, whether the immigrant is documented or not.

Language and cultural barriers also serve as roadblocks to safety. As a result, some immigrant victims often don't know their rights, how to gain access to services, or how to work with police.

Batterers exert control. Many deliberately give their victims misinformation about the laws. Abusers often keep control of immigration documents, and threaten their victims with deportation or loss of access to children if domestic violence is reported.

Lesbian, Gay, Bisexual, Transgender Community

The same issues of power and control can be present in the whole continuum of relationships, no matter a person's sexual orientation or gender identity:

In a survey of men in gay relationships, the lifetime prevalence of domestic violence was 39.2%. And 22% of men reported physical abuse in the last five years.

Women with Disabilities

Women with disabilities, including mental illness, and deaf women are at greater risk for intimate partner violence than women without disabilities. Not only does their disability make them more vulnerable, the barriers to seeking safety can be higher.

An abuser can utilize many tactics to keep a partner with disabilities under control. These range from manipulation of medication to refusal to help meet basic needs to destruction of adaptive equipment.

Mobility and accessibility barriers may keep a woman with disabilities from leaving an intimate partner or reporting violence.

Again, fear is a significant factor. Fear of losing independence and fear of losing vital support can keep a woman in an abusive relationship.

Women with disabilities tend to stay in dangerous relationships longer than their counterparts without disabilities: 11.3 years versus 7.1 years in situations of physical abuse, for example.

Elderly Women

The challenge to assist elderly women facing abusive relationships may escalate as the "baby boom" generation begins to enter old age. Today, it is estimated that:

More than one in ten women over 50 suffers from physical, sexual, or verbal abuse perpetrated by an intimate partner.

Abuse of elderly women by their spouses is growing among the "over 60" demographic in the United States.

Advocates have identified two categories of domestic violence against the elderly:

Domestic violence grown old – this is a pattern of violence that continues into old age.

Late onset domestic violence – this begins in old age, and may be linked to challenges surrounding retirement, disabilities, new roles for family members, or sexual changes.

The symptoms are the same as those associated with physical or sexual abuse in younger women. Other characteristics of domestic violence against elderly women include:

- Injuries occur more often and become more severe over time.
- Victims often experience intense confusion and disassociation.
- The violence is preceded by periods of intense tension, which are followed by periods of apparent contrition on the part of the abuser.

Employees/Colleagues

Domestic Violence is a business issue that cannot be ignored. Many people facing domestic violence spend at least eight hours a day in the workplace. Domestic violence affects employee health and well-being, productivity, benefits, costs, and engenders risk to the employer. It is therefore important that employees who are victims or perpetrators and employers notice the signs and find ways of dealing with the situation.

Lesson 48: Process Group – What Have You Learned About Yourself?

The following questions are meant to help you self-reflect and see what progress you have made on your road to recovery from domestic abuse. Be honest with yourself as you answer the following questions:

1. What have you learned about yourself through this process so far?

2. What have been your biggest challenges so far? What have been your biggest successes?

3. Are you being honest with others? How has that been demonstrated?

4. How is your family life? How emotionally healthy are your personal relationships?

5. What current stressors do you have in your life and how are you managing them?

6. What temptations have you struggled with lately? How have you dealt with these temptations?

7. How have you been dishonest?

8. What have been your successes?

9. What are you grateful for?

Lesson 49: Thinking Errors

Note: This lesson is a long one and will take three sessions to complete.

Here are some descriptions of some common problematic thinking patterns as described by G.K. Simon in the book, *Character Disturbance*:

Egocentric Thinking – A person with a character disturbance is almost always concerned with and for himself. Whatever the situation, it is always about him. He frequently finds himself thinking about things that he wants, because that is what is important to him. He hardly ever thinks about what someone else might want or need, because he attaches so little importance to that. Because he thinks the entire world revolves around him, he believes it is the duty of others to place what he desires or what interests him above everything else.

When he wants something, he does not consider whether or not it's right or good, or if his pursuit of it might adversely affect someone else; he only cares that he wants it. His constant concern for himself and the things he desires promotes an attitude of indifference to the rights, needs, wants, or experiences of others.

This type of attitude fosters a complete disregard for social obligation. In some cases, there is an ardent disdain for and total refusal to accept obligation.

He believes the world owes him everything and that he owes the world nothing. Such thinking is the reason the disturbed character develops an attitude of entitlement.

He has extremely high expectations for everyone else, but feels no sense that he should submit himself to the expectations of theirs or the society in general. His egocentric thinking patterns, attitudes, and their resultant behaviors prompt him to lead an extremely self-centered lifestyle.

- How have you demonstrated an attitude of self-centeredness in your life?
- What self-centered expectations do you have about others?
- How has self-centeredness hurt your relationships?

Possessive Thinking – People with character disturbances tend to view their relationships as possessions that they rightfully own; they should be able to do as they wish with these people. This type of thinking frequently accompanies *Heartless Thinking*.

Heartless Thinking – The heartless thinker tends to objectivity others (that is, he sees others as mere objects or pawns to manipulate for one's own purposes, rather than as individuals with whom one has to form a co-equal relationship).

Both possessive thinking and heartless thinking promote a dehumanizing attitude. This makes it more likely that the disturbed character will view others, not as human beings, but as objects of pleasure, vehicles to get things he wants, or simply potential obstacles to his path that must be removed.

Possessive and heartless thinking make it all but impossible for the person possessing these characteristics to view others as individuals with rights, needs, boundaries, or desires of their own, and beings of dignity worthy of respect and consideration.

Such thinking is carried to a most pathological extreme in the *psychopath personality*.

- Have you ever viewed others as objects or possessions? If so, how? How has this affected your relationships?
- Are you able to collaborate and cooperate with others? Do you demonstrate care and concern for others' points of view?

Extreme (All Or Nothing) Thinking—Abusive people tend to see things in terms of black and white, all-or-nothing. They might take the position that, if they can't have all that they ask for; then they won't accept anything.

If someone doesn't agree with everything they say then they will frame it as not being valued or listened to at all.

If they don't see themselves completely on top and in total control, then they will cast themselves as being on the bottom and under someone else's thumb.

This erroneous way of thinking makes it virtually impossible for them to develop any reasonable sense of give and take in their relationships. It promotes an uncompromising attitude that impairs their ability to develop any sense of moderation in their behavior patterns.

- How have you demonstrated all-or-nothing thinking in your life?
- Are you able to see "grey" areas in every situation, or do you find yourself being polarized in your thinking?

Inattentive Thinking – Some researchers describe this type of thinking error as the "mental filter" because abusive characters selectively filter what goes on around them, paying attention to and heeding only to the things they want to pay attention to, while disregarding all the rest.

They only hear what they want to rear, remember what they want to remember, and learn what they want to learn. They invest themselves intensely in the things that interest them; but they actively disregard the things they don't care about, even though they may be quite aware that others want them to pay more attention to these things.

They use the responsibility-avoidance tactic of selective attention. They "tune out" someone who's trying to teach them a lesson or only half listen whenever they hear something they don't like. They do this most often when others are urging them to submit themselves to the pro-social values and standards of contact. This erroneous way thinking is a major reason they develop both lackadaisical antisocial attitudes. In turn, their devil-may-care and antisocial attitudes predispose them to chronic and unyielding behaviors that conflict with major social norms.

- How have you demonstrated selective listening in your life?
- How often do you "tune people out" when you don't feel like listening to them?
- What are you willing to do to change yourself if you demonstrate this type of thinking?

Deceptive (Wishful) Thinking – Some people with abusive tendencies are prone to see things as they want to see them instead of as they really are. Two core personal characteristics contribute to this type of thinking:

1. The ease with which they lie.

2. Their resistance to demands placed on them by their environments.

This type of thinking involves the willingness to distort reality. It's not that they don't know the truth, but that they simply don't want reality to get in the way of what they want. They lie to themselves with the same ease that they lie to others.

They alter their perceptions and distort the reality of situations so they don't have to alter their stance, change their point of view, or question their usual way of doing things.

Sometimes they live ina world of their own fantasy, adhering to the belief that "thinking makes it so." Their determination to make reality what they want it to be breeds a pervasive attitude of disregard for the truth.Self-deceptive thinking is not the same thing as denial. The latter is an unconscious defense against unbearable emotional pain. Deliberate, self-serving twisting of facts and misrepresentations are bad habits for sure, as well as ways to avoid responsibility; but they're not the result of an altered psychological state.

People who demonstrate this type of thinking can often be quite convincing as they protest how; "I don't need help with anger management, I don't really have a problem here". He might make this type of assertion despite a virtual mountain of evidence to the contrary. He might maintain the assertion that there are no problems in his relationships despite the litany of evidence demonstrating decades of broken relationships.

Does he actually not see the problem? Actually, most of the time he sees it just fine; but he isn't motivated to deal with it or change it, so he tries to justify himself and get others off his back by suggesting there is no problem.

Other times, he's lied so much that he believes his own lies. Still other times, he has twisted and distorted so many aspects of life's realities that he can't tell what's real anymore.

- What are some of the areas of your life where you have used deceptive thinking?
- How have you tried to use this technique to minimize your problems, distort the truth, or not deal with something others deem important?
- **Impulsive Thinking** – Some people with abusive tendencies think primarily about what they want in the moment. They don't bother to think long-range or about the likely eventual consequences of their behavior. They lack prudence.

They act first and sometimes think afterwards (but not always.) Sometimes they never regret their impulsive acts, some, however, do experience after-the-fact regret. It depends on how negatively their actions impact their own priorities in life.

People who demonstrate this type of thinking often do not spend time thinking about the potential impact of their behavior before they act. They think only about what they want and how to get it now. This type of thinking predisposes them to think in the short-range and ignore potential long-range consequences. This also promotes a "devil-may-care," lackadaisical attitude, and attitudes of indifference, uncaring, or nonchalance.

- What types of impulsive actions can you think of that you have taken in the past?
- How has impulsivity impacted your sense of responsibility and maturity?
- What impulsive actions have you taken in the past that have caused you regret? What changes have you made when faced with regret?
- What can you do from this point forward to eliminate impulsive tendencies in yourself?

Prideful Thinking – People with prideful thinking often live by the slogan, "Image is everything." This, in fact, can be a core belief for some people with abusive tendencies. In some cases it becomes pathologically extreme.

Many abusive people think that there is nothing worse than admitting a mistake, backing down, or giving in, because it makes them look inadequate or "weak." They place their image above everything else. They think in such prideful ways that their ability to develop relationships based on mutual regard is extremely impaired. Instead of acknowledging shortcomings or errors and correcting a course, they resist change while engaging in a wide variety of behaviors designed to manage the impression others have of them. They often will not concede, even when they know full well they are off base.

One important reason for engaging in "impression management" is those who do don't want anyone to know who they really are. They do not want a level interpersonal "playing field." They cannot bear the thought of being on level ground with others in relationships, and are only comfortable in the "one up" position.

Habitual prideful thinking promotes the development of vanity and attitudes of haughtiness, arrogance, and pretentiousness. Thinking he can never really acknowledge a mistake prevents the person with this tendency from profiting from experiencing, especially when life is trying to teach him a lesson.

Before people can really correct problem patterns of behavior, they have to humbly admit they have a problem. To admit a problem is to acknowledge a shortcoming. Prideful thinking is a major barrier to recognizing or correcting any of the many problematic social behaviors common to an abusive person.

- How have you been prideful, arrogant, or pretentious?
- In what areas of your life are you willing to admit you have problems?
- How can humility help you overcome pride?
- What must you personally overcome in order to demonstrate true humility (teachability) in your life?

Unreasonable Thinking– Some people with abusive tendencies are very unrealistic in their thinking about life and the world around them. They also tend to harbor excessive expectations. But, their unreasonable views and expectations are usually very one-sided. They tend to set virtually unattainable standards for everyone else, while feeling no concomitant sense of obligation to meet the general social expectations most of us would like them to accept.

Abusive people expect a whole lot from their government, their bosses, their spouses and children, and anyone else who has any kind of relationship with them. And those expectations are almost always ridiculously irrational.

They expect things to go their way – all the time. They expect a lot of everyone, usually putting considerable stress on their relationships.

People with this distorted belief have no sense of balance, fairness, or compromise. Thinking so unreasonably eventually leads them to develop a rigidly demanding attitude. The unreasonable demands they bring to a relationship are a most frequent source of conflict and relationship distress. A partner might try to reason with them to no avail. Their thinking is too focused on their own expectations of others to be refocused on what they might do differently to get their wants and needs met.

The burden for changing this type of thinking rests squarely on the shoulders of the beholder.

- Ask people closest to you what unreasonable demands you have placed on them. What are you willing to acknowledge? What are you willing to change?
- How have you been disappointed, hurt, and angry over the unmet expectations you have placed on others?

Irrelevant Thinking – Abusive people often focus on the small, petty aspects of situations, but ignore the most important things, or the "big picture." They will take issue with their boss, the government, or with their partners on trivialities while not paying any attention to the things that really matter.

When someone confronts them on their behavior, they will get hung-up on a "technicality" or small inaccuracy while ignoring the larger truth. Their habitual attention to things not really relevant leads them to develop attitudes of pettiness and thoughtlessness.

- Discuss how irrelevant thinking has impacted your life?
- What types of "hills" have you been willing to "die" on?

Victim Mentality – Abusers often portray themselves as victims of circumstances or others' actions, rather than as persons responsible for their own actions and consequences of those actions. They frequently sit on their "pity-pots," feeling sorry for themselves and the "raw deals" they imagine they have been dealt in life.

This type of thinking leads to attitudes of bitterness and resentment. It is one of the reasons why abusers frequently enter relationships with a fairly substantial chip already on their shoulders.

- Write a list of your resentments.
- Now, write a list of your part in each resentment.

Lesson 50: Empathy

I Don't Feel Your Pain: Overcoming Roadblocks to Empathy

Written by: David F. Swink

Why empathy is important at home and work, and how to be better at it

What is Empathy?

According to emotional intelligence author, Daniel Goleman, empathy is defined as (1) understanding the emotional makeup of people and (2) treating people according to their emotional reactions. Goleman and other emotional intelligence and workplace competency researchers have consistently identified empathy as a core component of emotional intelligence and a powerful predictor of success in many professions. Empathy helps us to develop deep levels of rapport and trust.

Having poor empathy skills can lead to serious consequences. It can lead to conflict born of misunderstanding. Without it we can feel lonely within a relationship. Lack of empathy can cause companies to make catastrophic blunders that alienate their customers or employees and it can even incite violence.

The Importance of Empathy

Recent research conducted at Massachusetts General Hospital has shown solid evidence that physician empathy plays an important role in forging strong patient-physician relationships and boosting patient satisfaction as well as patients having better treatment adherence and suffering from fewer major medical errors.

Empathy is also important in the workplace. A study conducted by the Center for Creative Leadership investigated 6,731 leaders from 38 countries. Their results reveal that empathy is positively related to job performance. The study concluded that managers who show more empathy toward direct reports are viewed as better performers in their job by their bosses.

Our Brains on Empathy

Neuroscientists have recently discovered that humans are wired to experience empathy through multiple systems of mirror neurons in our brains. These mirror neurons reflect back actions that we observe in others causing us to mimic that action in our own brains. When we observe someone in pain or when we are with someone happy, we experience that to a certain extent. These mirror neurons are the primary physiological basis of empathy. They create a neural Wi-Fi that connects us to the feelings of people around us.

Many people seem to be naturally empathetic. Others are not. The good news is that research shows that empathy can be learned. There are however a few potential roadblocks to empathy that must be overcome.

Overcoming Roadblocks to Empathy

Roadblock 1:

Not Paying Attention

Mirror neurons kick in strongest when we observe a person's emotions. We see facial expressions, eye expressions, body position, and gestures. We may lack motivation to pay attention to a person or we may be too distracted by our own thoughts or by other things around us while we are multi-tasking.

The Solution:

Motivate yourself to be more empathetic by knowing how important empathy is to success at home and work. Put your PDA and computer away and minimize distractions. Learn about and practice active listening.

Fine tune your nonverbal observation skills. Learn about micro-expressions (small quick facial expressions) and eye reading. Daniel Goleman in his book, Social Intelligence, states that "the more sharply attentive we are, the more keenly we will sense another person's inner state."

Watch TV with the volume down and practice your nonverbal interpretation by reading what each character is feeling and talking about. This is best done with subtle dramas, not action movies.

Roadblock 2

Feeling the emotion of the other person but not knowing how or when to communicate empathetically.

The Solution:

Increase your awareness about your own non-verbal expressions (eyes and micro-expressions). Notice what you are doing nonverbally when you are interacting with others. Ask people that you trust to give you honest feedback about your non-verbal communication in various situations especially ones that are more emotional.

Notice with whom you have difficulty being empathetic. Examine why.

Learn more about voice tone. Listen to people who are known as empathetic leaders, teachers, friends, politicians, or even TV interviewers. Listen to how they use their voices to express empathy.

Try saying the sentence: "I'm sorry that happened to you," several different ways with various voice tones. See if you can tell which sounds most empathetic or ask someone else to give you feedback.

Recognize that there are some situations where it may be counterproductive to respond empathetically, such as when a person is sending signals that they don't want to interact with you or they don't want to share with you how they are feeling.

Roadblock 3

Not feeling the same emotion the other person is feeling but knowing intellectually that you need to communicate empathetically.

This is known as cognitive empathy.

The Solution:

Know that you can disagree with someone and still understand what they may be feeling and why. This is especially important when someone is having a strong emotion and is asking you to do something that you can't do.

Sometimes just listening without judgment is enough to convey cognitive empathy. Communicate to the person in an authentic way that you understand what they are experiencing.

Can you fake being empathetic?

Sometimes it may be necessary to act empathetically to achieve a desired outcome even when you feel antagonistic to a person. I have trained hostage negotiators for many years. Hostage negotiators are trained to act empathetically toward the hostage taker in order to establish the rapport necessary to influence him to give up and not hurt anyone. In fact, the negotiator most likely despises a person that would hold a woman and baby as hostages. What is interesting is that after a couple of hours many negotiators actually start to feel some empathy toward the hostage taker as a result of "acting" empathetic. Most of us will never find ourselves in that position, but you may need to fake empathy to influence someone to an important end. Hopefully, you won't experience that frequently, because there is often a price to pay for being consistently inauthentic.

Empathy is one of the building blocks of social intelligence. Stress, self-absorption, and lack of time can gang up on empathy to kill it. Knowing what your empathy roadblocks are and exploring ways to overcome them can help you develop a tool that is vital to your success at home and work.

Do you believe people can increase their ability to be empathetic?

Have you increased your empathy skills or helped others to do it? How?

What impact do you believe empathy plays in the workplace?

Do you think some people are too empathetic?

Lesson 51: Being In A Healthy Relationship

Read the following statements and apply them to your current relationship or a previous relationship. See areas where improvement is needed.

Written by: Alice Boyes

What you know and like about your partner should tell you a lot.

If you can say yes to most of these, it's very likely you're in a healthy relationship:

1. You can name your partner's best friend and identify a positive quality that the person has.
2. You and your partner are playful with each other.
3. You think your partner has good ideas.
4. You'd like to become more like your partner, at least in some ways.
5. Even when you disagree, you can acknowledge your partner makes sensible points.
6. You think about each other when you're not physically together.
7. You see your partner as trustworthy.
8. In relationship-relevant areas such as warmth and attractiveness, you view your partner a little bit more positively than they view themselves or than most other people view them.
9. You enjoy the ways your partner has changed and grown since you met.
10. Your partner is enthusiastic when something goes right for you.
11. When you reunite at the end of the day, you say something positive before you say something negative.
12. You reminisce about positive experiences you've had together in the past.
13. You can name one of your partner's favorite books.
14. You know your partner's aspirations in life.
15. You can recall something you did together that was new and challenging for both of you.
16. You kiss every day.
17. You're comfortable telling your partner about things that make you feel vulnerable such as worries about getting laid off.
18. You have your own "love language" (pet names or special signs you give each other).
19. You know your partner's most embarrassing moment from childhood.
20. You know your partner's proudest moment from childhood.
21. You never, or very rarely, express contempt for your partner by rolling your eyes, swearing at them, or calling them crazy.

22. You can list some positive personality qualities your partner inherited from their parents.

23. If you have children together, you can list some positive personality qualities your partner has passed on to your children.

24. You enjoy supporting your partner's exploration of personal goals and dreams, even when this involves you staying home.

25. You have a sense of security: you're confident your partner wouldn't be unfaithful, or do something to jeopardize your combined financial security.

26. When you argue, you still have a sense that your partner cares about your feelings and opinions.

27. Your partner lets you into his/her inner emotional world—he/she makes his/her thoughts and feelings accessible to you.

28. You frequently express appreciation for each other.

29. You frequently express admiration for each other.

30. You feel a sense of being teammates with your partner.

31. You know your partner's favorite song.

32. You have a sense that your individual strengths complement each other.

33. When you say goodbye in the morning, it's mindful and affectionate.

34. If you've told your partner about trauma you've experienced, they've reacted kindly.

35. You don't flat-out refuse to talk about topics that are important to your partner.

36. You respect your partner's other relationships with family or friends, and view them as important.

37. You have fun together.

38. You see your partner's flaws and weaknesses in specific rather than general ways. (For example, you get annoyed about them forgetting to pick up the towels, but you don't generally see them as inconsiderate).

39. You're receptive to being influenced by your partner; you'll try their suggestions.

40. You're physically affectionate with each other.

41. You enjoy spending time together.

42. You feel a zing when you think about how you first met.

43. You can name your partner's favorite relative.

44. You can name your partner's most beloved childhood pet.

45. You can articulate what your partner sees as the recipe for happiness.

46. When you feel stressed or upset, you turn toward your partner for comfort, rather than turning away from your partner and trying to deal with it yourself.

47. You have a sense that it's easy to get your partner's attention if you've got something important to say.

48. You like exploring your partner's body.

49. You can name your partner's favorite food.

50. If you could only take one person to a deserted island, you'd take your partner.

Now, here are some advices by another author on how to choose a healthy partner. Since this is a batterer's intervention program, use the information both ways to evaluate the type of partner you need to choose and also the type of partner you need to be in order to have a healthy relationship.

Lesson 52: How to Choose a Healthy Partner

(Source: Lena Aberdene Derhally)

1. **Don't make choices out of fear:** so many times people either choose a partner or stay with someone in an unhappy relationship predominantly out of some kind of fear. Usually that fear is being alone but fears can vary widely from person to person. It's often better to be alone and wait for the right person than to make a decision out of fear. Making decisions out of fear leads to confusion, anxiety and a general feeling of something being amiss.

2. **Be careful of jumping into a committed relationship right off the bat:** it can be tempting to jump into a committed relationship quickly when you find someone you have a fiery connection with. However, you don't really know that person yet and you're getting emotionally invested in someone that you don't know much about. As time progresses, you may find out things that you really don't like or that you're truly not compatible with this person. Because you invested so much emotional energy quickly, this can hurt a lot more than it would have if you had taken time to get to know the person before putting your whole heart into the relationship. When we're in the "romantic" stages of the beginning of a relationship, we are often making choices out of lust and fantasy-like projections, instead of reality and logic. It's important to remain grounded and patient when deciding to be seriously committed to someone.

3. **Give people a chance that you normally wouldn't give a chance to:** if I had a dime for every time someone told me they weren't going to go out with someone because they weren't their "type," I'd be a rich woman! Remember attraction can grow the more you get to know a person and their personality. Some people also take a lot of time to get to know and don't wear their heart on their sleeves. Still waters run deep and you may not get a chance to find that out if you don't take the time to get to know someone.

4. **Throw out your checklist:** Many people have extensive lists of what qualities and traits their ideal partner has to have. If you box yourself into a checklist, you may miss out on some great matches for you. It's almost impossible to find a perfect checklist partner, and when we think we have found it we throw all caution to the wind and disregard some not so desirable qualities. A great relationship has emotional compatibility. How does the person make you feel as opposed to what this person looks like on paper?

5. **Look for qualities that are the foundation of a good partnership, throw the tiny details out:** the qualities of a person that help to build the foundation of a good partnership are: empathy, integrity, honesty, reliability, kindness and emotional generosity. If you find these qualities in someone, be curious about pursuing it further, even if they may not seem like your type on the surface. Other criteria like "sense of humor," "world traveler," and "good dancer" are nice-to-

haves but don't necessarily have to be there for you to be happy in your relationship.

6. **Don't let lust be your guide:** people have a tendency to put up with a lot of crap from someone they are dating when they feel a magnetic chemistry with them. Magnetic chemistry has a strong power because it isn't something that happens often. When we find someone we have magnetic chemistry with, not only is it an aphrodisiac that we can't get enough of, but we also confuse it with the right person (e.g., "this must be right if I feel this strongly!"). Magnetic chemistry is great but don't excuse bad behavior because of it.

7. **Don't confuse an "emotional roller coaster" with being crazy about someone:** when someone isn't fully emotionally available to us or we don't know where they stand, it creates a type of anxiety. The anxiety has a way of taking over our brains to the point where our thoughts are all consumed by this person. We're constantly thinking about where they are and what they are doing. Before we know it, we start planning our lives around them. Maybe you decide to keep your calendar open just so you don't miss an opportunity to see this person. When the person validates and affirms you, it feels great! On the flip side, when they remove themselves emotionally, ignore, manipulate or berate, it feels like the worst thing in the world. Soon the relationship has turned into a see-saw of high-highs and low-lows, which can make us feel a bit crazy or out of our element. Don't confuse these types of feelings with love.

8. **Find someone you can be yourself around:** this may sound cliched but it's true. Picking a partner where you feel like you can be 100 percent yourself with no judgment and complete acceptance is a wonderful and liberating feeling. In life it can be difficult to find avenues where you can truly be yourself. A relationship should be your safe and comfortable place where you don't have to keep a mask on.

9. **Don't keep waiting for something to change that obviously won't:** the longer you stay in a situation that you know is ultimately doomed or doesn't align with your personal values, the more you block yourself from having the opportunity to meet the right person. Be clear with yourself about what you will and won't accept and know what your deal-breakers are. Once you become clear on those things, it is easier to make a decision about the fate of a relationship.

10. **Have fun!** The less pressure you put on yourself, the happier you are with yourself, and the more at ease you are, it will create a space to attract the right kind of people to you. Sometimes it takes seeing a lot of what you don't want to figure out what you do want. Enjoy yourself!

Homework Assignment:

Read the above two lists and see areas in your life that need to change. Be prepared to share with group members at next meeting.

References

AVA (n.d.) *Dynamics of Domestic Violence.* Retrieved from http://ava-online.org/lessons/lesson-03/

Bancroft, L. (Winter 2002). *The batterer as a parent.* Synergy, 6(1), 6-8. (Newsletter of the National Council of Juvenile and Family Court Judges)

Bancroft, L. (2007). *Checklist for Assessing Change in Men who Abuse Women.* Retrieved from: http://lundybancroft.com/articles/checklist-for-assessing-change-in-men-who-abuse-women/

Bancroft, L. (n.d.). *Guide for Men who are Serious about Changing – Part 1.* Retrieved from http://lundybancroft.com/articles/guide-for-men-who-are-serious-about-changing-part-1/

Bancroft, L. (n.d.). *Guide for Men who are Serious about Changing – Part 2.* Retrieved from http://lundybancroft.com/articles/guide-for-men-who-are-serious-about-changing-part-2/

Bancroft, L. (2005) *Story of Emotional Injury and Recovery in Children Exposed to Domestic Abuse.* Retrieved fromhttp://lundybancroft.com/articles/a-story-of-emotional-injury-and-recovery-in-children-exposed-to-domestic-abuse/

Barnette, V. (n.d.) *How to Communicate Assertively and Respectfully.* Retrieved from http://www.uwosh.edu/ccdet/caregiver/Documents/Gris/Handouts/gracasr.pdf

Beck, A. T. (1976). *Cognitive therapies and emotional disorders.* New York: New American Library.

Beck Institution (n.d.) *What is Cognitive Behavior Therapy?* Retrieved from https://www.beckinstitute.org/get-informed/what-is-cognitive-therapy/

Burns, D. D. (1980). *Feeling good: The new mood therapy.* New York: New American Library.

CCWRC (n.d.) *About Domestic Violence.* Retrieved from: http://ccwrc.org/about-abuse/about-domestic-violence/

Cheng, K. T. (2016). *9 Ways to be Accountable When You've Been Abusive*. Retrieved from http://everydayfeminism.com/2016/02/be-accountable-when-abusive/

Delaware Coalition Against Domestic Violence (n.d.) *Who is Affected by Domestic Violence?* Retrieved from http://www.dcadv.org/who-affected-domestic-violence

Derhally, L.A. (2016) *10 Tips for Choosing the Right Partner.* Retrieved from http://www.huffingtonpost.com/lena-aburdene-derhally/choosing-right-partner_b_7688382.html

Durve, A (2012). *The Power to Break Free Workbook.* U.S.A.: The Power to Break Free Foundation.

Edleson, J.L. (2012, November*). Groupwork with Men Who Batter: What the Research Literature Indicates.* Harisburg, PA: VAWnet, a project of the National Resource Center on Domestic Violence.

Grohol, J. M., (n.d.) *15 Common Cognitive Distortions.* Retrieved from https://psychcentral.com/lib/15-common-cognitive-distortions/

Grohol, J. M., (n.d.) Fixing Cognitive Distortions. Retrieved from https://psychcentral.com/lib/fixing-cognitive-distortions/

James, J. (2017). The Grief Recovery Handbook, 20th Anniversary Expanded Edition: The Action Program for Moving Beyond Death, Divorce, and Other Losses including Health, Career, and Faith. New York: NY: Harper Collins

Los Angeles Police Department (n.d.) *Domestic Violence: Understanding the Cycle of Violence.* http://lapdonline.org/get_informed/content_basic_view/8878

Lee, J. (1993). *Facing the Fire: Experiencing and Expressing Anger Appropriately.* New York, NY: Bantam Books.

Loveisrespect.org (n.d.) *What is Emotional Abuse/Verbal Abuse?* Retrieved from http://www.loveisrespect.org/pdf/What_Is_Emotional_Verbal_Abuse.pdf

Mind Tools (n.d.) *Emotional Intelligence: Developing Strong "People Skills"* Retrieved from https://www.mindtools.com/pages/article/newCDV_59.htm

Montero, M.D. Is History Repeating Itself in Your Relationships? Retrieved from http://www.huffingtonpost.com/mary-montero/is-history-repeating-itse_b_672518.html

OC Probation Deptment (2017). *Batterers' Intervention Program Standards and Procedures.* Orange County, CA: OC Probation Department.

Pope, L. & Ferraro, K. (2006). The Duluth Power and Control Model. Flagstaff, AZ: Collaborative Consulting.

Simon, G.K. (2011).*Character Disturbance: The Phenomenon of Our Age.* Little Rock, AK: Parkhurst Brothers, Inc., Publishers

Spradlin, S.E. (2003). *Don't Let Your Emotions Run Your Life: How Dialectical Behavior Therapy Can Put You in Control.* Oakland, CA: Harbinger Publications, Inc

Storkey, C. (2017). *Listening Skills – 11 Steps to Become a Good Listener.* Retrieved from http://calebstorkey.com/listening-skills-11-steps-to-become-a-good-listener/

Swink, D. F. (2013). *I Don't Feel Your Pain: Overcoming Roadblocks to Empathy.* Retrieved from https://www.psychologytoday.com/blog/threat-management/201303/i-dont-feel-your-pain-overcoming-roadblocks-empathy

World Health Organization (WHO) (n.d.) *Changing Cultural and Social Norms that Support Violence.* Retrieved from http://www.who.int/violence_injury_prevention/violence/norms.pdf

Made in the USA
Coppell, TX
20 August 2023

20553967R00090